EDWARD ROSE

Negro Trail Blazer

Other Books by Harold W. Felton

LEGENDS OF PAUL BUNYAN

PECOS BILL: TEXAS COWPUNCHER

JOHN HENRY AND HIS HAMMER

FIRE-FIGHTIN' MOSE

BOWLEG BILL: SEAGOING COWPUNCHER

COWBOY JAMBOREE: WESTERN SONGS AND LORE

NEW TALL TALES OF PECOS BILL

MIKE FINK: BEST OF THE KEELBOATMEN

THE WORLD'S MOST TRUTHFUL MAN

A HORSE NAMED JUSTIN MORGAN

SERGEANT O'KEEFE AND HIS MULE, BALAAM

WILLIAM PHIPS AND THE TREASURE SHIP

PECOS BILL AND THE MUSTANG

JIM BECKWOURTH, NEGRO MOUNTAIN MAN

EDWARD ROSE
Negro Trail Blazer

By *Harold W. Felton*

ILLUSTRATED WITH PHOTOGRAPHS,

PRINTS OF THE PERIOD,

AND MAPS

DODD, MEAD & COMPANY

NEW YORK

Library of Congress Catalog Card Number: 67-21521

Printed in the United States of America
by The Cornwall Press, Inc., Cornwall, N. Y.

The reproductions of the Charles Bodmer prints and the Alfred Jacob
Miller watercolors from the Joslyn Art Museum, Omaha, Nebraska, are
from the Northern Natural Gas Company Collection. The George Catlin
oil, "Prairie Picnic," is from the Joslyn Art Museum Collection, gift of
M. Knoedler & Company, New York.

Maps by James MacDonald

For Josephine and Duke

Introduction

THE ancient fur trade with the Indians" was carried on by a "notable band of men . . . men of different races and colors and alike only in their energy, bravery and initiative."

This comment is made by Archer B. Hulbert in *The Paths of Inland Commerce*. It is often repeated in varying ways by other writers.

One of this notable band of men, one of the very first, was a Negro, Edward Rose. He was enterprising and brave enough to stand out in a rough and rugged world. It was a world no one entered who did not have those qualities in great abundance.

Edward Rose was a mountain man's mountain man, a trail blazer's trail blazer. He went up the Missouri River in 1807, the year after the return of Lewis and Clark. This was fifteen years before the first of the famous Ashley expeditions. He was a chief of the Crow Indians almost twenty years before another famous Negro, Jim Beckwourth, reached Absaroka, the home of the Crows.

Rose was already an experienced mountain man when most of the later and better known beaver trappers were still boys. Ed Rose was an old hand at western exploration when men like William Ashley, Kit Carson, Jim Bridger, Jim Beckwourth, Tom Fitzpatrick, and Jed Smith first went to the mountains. He was their guide and interpreter. He showed them the way when they first turned their faces toward the Rockies.

The late comers, but still early explorers, sought him out. They and their biographers were not all kind to his memory, but it is evident that his critics did not know or did not tell his whole story.

Common superlatives seem inadequate to express how important the trail blazers were to the nation and the remarkable part they played in history. It was, as Kenneth A. Spaulding observes in his introduction to Alexander Ross' *Fur Hunters of the Far West,* "an era as adventurous as any our continent has known."

George Frederick Ruxton, an Englishman who traveled extensively in the West in the middle 1840's, wrote of the early trappers and traders. His work first appeared as a series for *Blackwood's Magazine* in 1848 and later was published as a book, *Life in the Far West.* He said: "These, nevertheless, were the men whose hardy enterprise opened to commerce and the plow the vast and fertile regions of the West. Rough and savage though they were, they were the true pioneers of that extraordinary tide of civilization which has poured its restless current through tracts large enough for kings to govern. . . . To the wild and half-savage trapper, who may be said to exemplify the energy, enterprise, and hardihood characteristic of the American people . . . to these men alone is due the empire of the West, destined in a few short years to become the most important of those confederated States comprising the mighty Union of North America."

Dale Lowell Morgan, in *The West of William Ashley,* considers Edward Rose's time to be ever more luminously a "golden age," and observes that the energies unleashed "profoundly shaped the history of the West." Richard Edward Oglesby, in *Manuel Lisa,* points out that the "earlier era contains its share of larger-than-life figures like John Colter, Edward Rose, and others. . . ." That is probably as good a way as any to describe Edward Rose—larger than life.

Edward Rose is not a clearly etched character in the chronicles of the early West. History was not made to revolve around him, as it was around some of the others who wrote letters and narratives. He left no written record of his adventures. But Rose made history. He was there, Johnny-on-the-spot, at almost every first and major step taken in the early, early West.

It is not known where he was born, or precisely when, where, or how he died, a fate he shares in common with many others in a land where uncounted men died alone, with their moccasins on and their guns in their hands. The people who keep statistics and write history were not around.

Rose had a way of showing up when and where he was needed. He went up the Missouri River with Manuel Lisa in 1807 in the first serious, large-scale trapping venture to the mountains. He went to the Yellowstone again in 1809 with Ezekial Williams, on the first all-land trip to the beaver country. He was an interpreter and guide for Wilson Price Hunt who led the Astorians westward in 1811. He was with another of Lisa's groups on a journey to the Yellowstone in 1812, and very likely he was with others in undocumented adventures.

His name sparkles to the surface in an incident which reveals that he was very much in demand and was doing a first-rate job. He was paid $250 in 1813 for guiding a trader, Lorimer, from Fort Union to the Crow Indians. There is a good deal of evidence of the quality of Ed Rose in this simple statement, and also of the high regard in which he was held. The Crows were five hundred to six hundred miles away, give or take a few hundred miles. It would require a month or so for such a trip. It would require a good deal of know-how, too, for the Crows moved their villages and no one knew exactly where they might be at any given time. All of this may be valued by comparing $250 with the ordinary pay of $300 a year for the full time of a beaver trapper. It may be recalled that in 1813 the Blackfeet and other Indians were supposedly being stirred up by the British as a part of the War of 1812. And of course it should not be forgotten that the Blackfeet and some of the others did not need anyone to stir them up. It was dangerous going. It took a good man.

There are only dim traces of Rose in and around the West during the next decade. In 1823, he stepped into the spotlight when he joined William Ashley and the men who were destined to become the "great and famous" mountain men. He was the guide and interpreter for some of those same young men on a trip to the mountains, the first trip for most of them.

He flashed into clear view again in 1825 when he was interpreter and guide for the Atkinson-O'Fallon treaty-making expedition to the Yellowstone. After that, we have occasional glimpses of him at his work during the greatest of the beaver-trapping days.

Edward Rose was a real man, with ramrod-steel bones, buckskin muscles, and calluses for nerves. His first biographer was Lieutenant Reuben Holmes who was with the Atkinson-O'Fallon expedition of 1825 and who obviously was greatly impressed by the Negro interpreter and guide. His work was first published in 1828 in the *St. Louis Beacon*. He made Rose a picaro, something of a rogue whose reputation was less than admirable, and his notions were later picked up by other writers.

Washington Irving wrote of Rose in *Astoria* and in *Adventures of Captain Bonneville*. David H. Coyner took notice of him in *The Lost Trappers* published in 1859. James Clyman saw Rose in action in 1823 and mentioned him in a narrative he wrote of his western experiences. Zenas Leonard gives us a good view of Rose as he was in 1833 and 1834 when he had a first-hand view of him. The journal of the Atkinson-O'Fallon expedition made a record of Rose's services as guide and interpreter. Colonel Henry Leavenworth noted Rose's superior work in a report of the battle with the Aricaras in 1823.

General Hiram Martin Chittenden, in his *A History of the American Fur Trade in the Far West,* which was written in 1902, included a couple of dozen biographies of men he considered important enough to the history of the fur trade to justify such distinction. Edward Rose was one of them.

Washington Irving saw Rose as "powerful in frame and fearless in spirit." Bernard De Voto finds Rose to be a man "with steel nerves and nine lives." To Colonel Henry Leavenworth, "he appeared to be a brave and enterprising man." Le Roy Hafen and W. J. Ghent call him a "dare-devil adventurer" and observed that "his incredible career makes the most adventurous fiction seem weak and pallid."

To Holmes' figure of a picaro, Irving added the unfounded suspicions of Wilson Price Hunt who feared treachery from Rose. Coyner followed suit. Many historians seem to have accepted their statements blindly and without question. But it is interesting that many of those who have noticed Ed Rose have seen through the shadows and have found him quite a different person.

Chittenden was able to peer through the early fictions and says, "It is apparent, therefore, that Rose bore a bad reputation, but the singular thing is that everything definite that is known of him is entirely to his credit. If judgment were to be passed only on the record as it has come down to us, he would stand as high as any character in the history of the fur trade."

Edgeley W. Todd, in a note in his edition of *Astoria*, comments of Rose, saying, "The bad light in which he appears in *Astoria* may not be justified." Bernard De Voto, in *Across the Wide Missouri*, similarly observes, "He had a reputation for treachery that appears not to have been deserved."

Charles L. Camp, in the *California Historical Society Quarterly*, points out that "most accounts of Rose are unsatisfactory" and he, too, corrects the early writers. "Yet even his worst enemies found his services invaluable during Indian troubles, and his bravery then as at other times often rose to the pitch of reckless foolhardiness. He has been called a renegade, but he nevertheless displayed gallantry which brought high praise from his commanders. . . .

"His great strength, desperate fearlessness, and intimate knowledge of Indian ways gained him such prestige among the Crows that he became virtually their chief."

All of this suggests that Edward Rose was a first-rate trail blazer and mountain man, guide and interpreter, motivated by conventional mountain-man urges. He was equal to the tasks faced by men entering a wild, unknown land, and facing warlike Indians who came to sense—and then to know—that it meant the end of their world.

Edward Rose lived for three decades in turmoil and adventure that have been the source of thousands of thrilling stories. The same three decades were the foundation for western expansion of Edward Rose's nation. He was an important part of it.

Illustrations

"Winter Village of the Minatarres," by Charles Bodmer
"View of the Rocky Mountains," by Charles Bodmer
"Indian Council," by Alfred Jacob Miller
"Indian Boy," by George Catlin

MAPS

1

No one knows where Edward Rose was born. No one knows where and how he spent his boyhood days. The names of his father and mother are lost, erased by time. But the record he made is to be found in the pages of history. It is a record made by a man's strength, determination, and skill, and his unquestioned courage.

Rose appears in the history of the early West the same year as an event of first importance. The earliest record of him is in 1806. Lewis and Clark returned to St. Louis in the flaming colors of autumn in 1806 after two years of exploration to the Pacific Ocean through an unknown land. Ed Rose played a leading role in most of the important expeditions to the Rocky Mountains in the next two decades. He was one of the earliest of the mountain men. He was the trail blazers' trail blazer.

He was muscular, thick set, but of good height. A big man. The color of his skin was black. His nose had been slashed in an accident or fight. The Indians called

him Cut Nose. To the French and Canadian trappers
and boatmen he was *Nez Coupé*. He bore a cruel scar
on his forehead. His eyes, dark and piercing, missed
nothing within their range. His mouth was firm, sel-
dom breaking into a sign of pleasure. He was a grim,
serious man, engaged in a grimly serious business.

Those who were in positions of influence sought him
out. Those in places of command were eager to accept
his services.

It was said he was born a slave. It was said that his
ancestors included Negro, white, and Cherokee, from
three continents—ancient Africa, old Europe, and new
America. If so, three continents had formed him, in the
American melting pot.

No written word of Edward Rose is preserved. He
may not have known how to write. In his world of early
western travel and adventure, many of the great trail
blazers had never been to school.

In many respects, his is an uncertain history. But
through the dim and often unclear record, the figure
of a man appears, a fiercely brave man, a fighter, a man
who was hated, admired, feared. Edward Rose was a
man who was trusted, and perhaps envied, who did his
job, his hard and dangerous job, and did it very well.

In the unknown western spaces, danger was at every
hand. The dark rivers, muddy with prairie soil, held
treacherous currents. On their banks and the grasslands
through which they flowed, in the rolling hills and

mountains of rock where they rose, cold and crystal clear, Indians lived whose trade was war. They were suspicious of strangers and they knew the ways of treachery. Knives and spears, bows, arrows, and guns were the tools of their trade. To take a scalp brought both pleasure and honor.

Not many men had the stomach for a life up the rivers so far from the comforts of home and the safety of the civilized and protected East. But some—a few— were drawn by the unknown. They were content to face new hazards each new day and each new night, and they were happy with adventure. Edward Rose was one of these, one of these very few.

2

Ed rose was in St. Louis in the spring of 1806 and spent the year in the company of some other hunters on the Osage River. He was fond of the hunter's life and he bargained with the trader, Manuel Lisa, in the spring of 1807, to ascend the Missouri River with him to the mouth of the Yellowstone.

History does not remember everyone in the same depth and, as with Rose, much of the early life of Manuel Lisa is not known. He was born in New Orleans in 1772, of Spanish parents, and was perhaps no more than eighteen years old when he went to St. Louis. He was in the fur trade with the Osage Indians in 1800, at the dawn of the nineteenth century.

None but the strong can succeed against the perilous currents of a wild river. None but the brave can face a dozen Indian tribes who live by the knife and the bow. None but the skillful can survive in a hostile land where a man lives on the game he can kill. Manuel Lisa was willing to accept the challenges, and Edward Rose was exactly the sort of man he needed for a venture into unknown lands.

Lisa had intelligence and the reckless bravery necessary in one of the most dangerous callings known to man, that of a trapper and mountain man in the early days of the West. Sydney Greenbie, in *Furs To Furrows*, says he had "bones that were flint and who struck them struck fire and burned his fingers."

Such words are often spoken of a leader, but they must also be said of the men who make such leadership possible, for they are the men with the guns in hand who must back up brave actions. Forty-two such men were in the group that went to the Yellowstone with Lisa in the spring of 1807. Among them were John Potts and Peter Wiser who had returned from the Pacific the year before with Lewis and Clark. Another was Edward Rose.

They were involved in the first attempt to engage in the fur trade on a large scale in the area around the headwaters of the Missouri. As the historian Hiram Martin Chittenden says in his book, *A History of the American Fur Trade in the Far West*, "It was a venture of no little hazard, for the destination was more than two thousand miles away, among tribes whose friendship was at least doubtful, and a goodly portion of the route lay through the country of other tribes already well known for their treacherous and desperate character."

A month after the party left St. Louis, it passed the
mouth of the Platte River. Here they met John Colter.
He, too, had been to the Pacific with Lewis and Clark.
He had left the explorers on the upper Missouri on
their return trip the year before. After a season of trapping, he was now returning to St. Louis on the spring
flood. John Colter would be another valuable man to
have, and he joined Lisa's group.

The keelboat they were dragging up the stream was
incredibly hard to manage in the erratic and shifting
river currents, which often ran close to shore within
easy reach of ball or arrow from hostile Indians. As
Chittenden says, "The lives of the party frequently
hung as upon a thread which the slightest maladroit-
ness or weakness would break."

When they reached the Aricaras in the present state
of South Dakota, ". . . that most treacherous of Indian
tribes," they were met by two or three hundred warriors who fired a volley across their bow. It was impossible to ignore their command, so they put to shore.
Women appeared with bags of corn to trade. An Indian
rushed up and cut the bags open. There was a scuffle.

It may have been a signal for attack. Lisa called his
men to arms and trained his two small swivel cannon
upon the shore. Indians knew the meaning of guns, and
they could understand the look of determination on the
faces of Ed Rose and the other men in the small group.
The expected attack did not come. Courage and

prompt action and the readiness to receive fire with fire prevented it.

A hundred miles farther north, the party passed the Mandan Indian villages without serious incident. The daily fight against the river continued to furnish them with work and excitement, but greater danger was always around the next bend. It came with the sight of a band of Assiniboiness. Four or five thousand Indians were gathered on the shore. It was no accident. All the way up the stream the news of the trappers' approach had always gone ahead of them, passed from one Indian tribe to another. The Assiniboines were there for business. The size of the band told the hunters clearly that they were bent on bad business.

Forty-two men on a heavy, difficult keelboat could be no match for such an Indian army. The trappers loaded their muskets and cannon and steered the boat directly toward the multitude on the shore.

Scalping knives, war clubs, spears, bows and arrows were waiting. As the keelboat approached the mob, scarcely a hundred yards away, all of the guns were fired, although they were aimed where no harm could be done. The Indians, shocked by the noise, flame, and smoke, fled for safety into the hills. A few braves and chiefs returned to smoke the peace pipe and receive presents, but the threat was gone.

The giving of presents was extremely important in dealing with Indians, and at every social or business meeting, friendship was expressed by exchanging gifts. The practice was not always freely followed, and an outnumbered group might be forced to give its goods and leave with a show of friendship, or refuse to make gifts and lose both goods and lives. Indians were not backward about asking for, or demanding, presents. The knowledge of when to give them, and what to give, and when not to give them, was necessary for a trapper. It was a talent Edward Rose possessed in abundance.

The trappers built Fort Lisa, or Fort Manuel, on the Yellowstone River at the mouth of the Big Horn. It was the first trading post established on the upper river and it was at the heart of Absaroka, the home of the Sparrow Hawk people, the Crows.

The Crows called themselves Absaroka and used the same word to describe the land in which they lived. Absaroka meant "Sparrow Hawk." The first French trappers translated it as *Corbeau* and the tribe, *les Corbeaux*. The French word was translated into English as Crow, and these Indians have since been known by that name.

The Crows were among the best horsemen of the Missouri valley Indians, and possessed more horses in proportion to their number than other tribes. They were tall, graceful, handsome, the best formed of the western Indians. They excelled most of the other tribes in

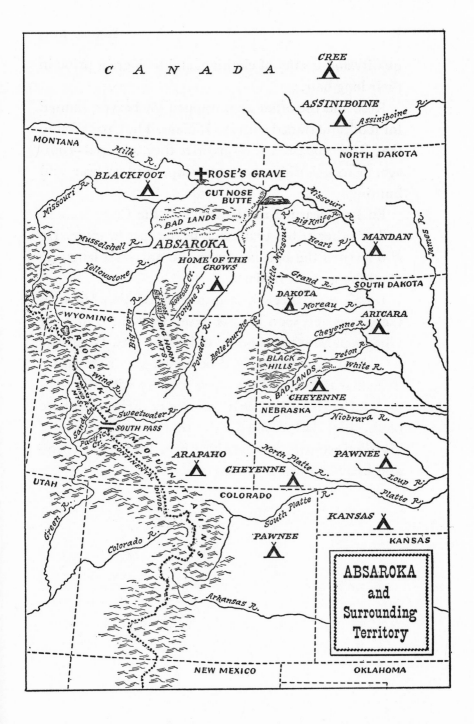

quality and beauty of clothing, and took great pride in their long hair.

Rose and the other men trapped for beaver, hunted for food, and traded with the Indians. The Crows found that Rose possessed the qualities they admired—courage, marksmanship, horsemanship, skill at war and hunting.

Ed Rose learned the language of the Crow Indians and of other tribes that came to the fort to trade. He also learned the sign language, the universal language of all the western Indians.

Rose's work threw him into close relationship with the Crows and soon he was living with them in their villages more often than he did at the fort. Gradually he gained their respect and became a man of great influence with them. They were friendly with the trappers, a fact that very likely was due to their acceptance of the big, dark-skinned Edward Rose and, later, of Jim Beckwourth, another Negro mountain man who also became a leader among them.

3

Much of the information we have of Edward Rose comes from Lieutenant Reuben Holmes. Holmes was born in Connecticut and was a graduate of the United States Military Academy. He was commissioned a second lieutenant of the 6th Infantry on July 1, 1823. Two years later he was a member of the Atkinson-O'Fallon expedition to the Yellowstone, the first successful treaty-making effort with the Missouri River Indians. Edward Rose was an interpreter with that group, and impressed the lieutenant to such an extent that the young offcer wrote a biographical sketch of him. It was first published in 1828 in the *St. Louis Beacon* and later appeared in the *St. Louis Reveille* in 1848.

There were five hundred men in the Yellowstone expedition, but the Negro trapper and trail blazer was the one who captured the young officer's imagination. Holmes may have received some of his information from the lips of Rose, but much of it appears to be prairie "shop talk," mountain-man yarns, and folklore.

Tales of heroism were often preserved by stories told around camp fires, and much of early western history comes to us in this fashion. Holmes heard many stories of Rose's adventures in this way in 1825. Many of the events had occurred almost twenty years before and had lived in the minds and on the tongues of mountain men for almost two decades.

One of the incidents in Holmes' story of Rose involves the practice of giving presents to Indians. Manuel Lisa and his small party needed the good will of the Crows. Gift-giving was one of the accepted ways of keeping Indian friends but, according to Holmes, Lisa thought Rose gave away too many presents. As a result, there were less goods to trade for furs and when Ed returned to the fort he did not have enough furs to please Lisa. There was a quarrel. As Holmes tells it:

"This quarrel took place between them in the counting room of the establishment, and almost at the moment of Mr. Lisa's departure—the boat, in fact, was waiting for him with the crew on their benches. They were alone, and during the dispute Rose sprang, like a tiger, upon his disputant, and overpowering him before he had noticed such an intention, would probably have killed him, had not the noise of the scuffle brought a man, by the name of Potts (since killed by the Blackfeet at the three forks of the Missouri—he was with Lewis and Clark in their voyage), to the relief of Mr. Lisa."

Lisa went to the waiting boat, but Rose was not through. He ran to the swivel cannon and pointed it toward the departing boat and touched it off. The result was near tragedy with a touch of frontier humor. Holmes says the cannon was touched off ". . . just as a man was passing in front of its muzzle. He happened to be a long-legged man, and in the act of stepping, so that a canister of bullets passed harmlessly between his legs, and only caused him to jump a few feet in the air and fall directly in front of the piece enveloped in smoke from which place he roared out that he was dead."

None of the boat's crew was injured, and apparently the incident was soon forgotten because Lisa, a few years later, was only too glad to see Ed Rose again. And even though Lisa thought Rose may have given too many presents to the Indians, the year's trade was satisfactory. Manuel Lisa returned to St. Louis in the spring of 1808 elated with his success. He continued the trade with a larger company the next year.

4

INDIANS often had more than one name, new names commonly coming to them through acts of unusual bravery. Lieutenant Holmes' tale of Edward Rose bears the title *The Five Scalps,* a name which Cut Nose was given during his stay with the Crows.

A small war party of eleven Minnatarees and a boy, their moccasin carrier, were camped in a wooded ridge overlooking a narrow valley. In the distance they saw a Crow warrior and his squaw approaching. Here were two scalps, welcome prizes for any war party. The Minnatarees concealed themselves "and strung their bows for the silent work of destruction."

The Crow couple passed before the concealed Indians. The ambush came. The sudden, soft twang of bow strings and the zip of arrows mixed with the songs of birds.

The Crow warrior reeled "in the dizziness of death," but the woman was not touched. She urged her horse on in another rain of arrows, and a shrieking band of

Minnatarees raised a cloud of dust behind her as her horse sped across the dry prairie.

The squaw had a good head start and was well mounted on a fine Crow pony. She out-distanced them, although a single arrow passed through her robe as it flapped in the air from her shoulders.

When the Minnatarees saw that she would escape, they returned to their camp, gathered up their goods, and pressed their tired horses to put this place of danger behind them. The squaw's Crow village would be near and Crow braves would be quick to seek revenge.

Upon reaching her village the squaw shouted out her story. The Crows—and Ed Rose, who was with them—responded with wild clamor. In a moment, Cut Nose and about fifty warriors were mounted. They dashed to the scene of the attack. The sight of the fallen Crow brave gave them a new lust for revenge. Holmes says that ". . . Rose, like the blood hound let loose from his chain, took the trail, followed by what would have been considered, by an inexperienced beholder, a troop of demons."

The chase went on for three hours, Cut Nose following a trail so thin it made the warriors wonder at his skill. The Crows, with superior horsemanship and fresh horses, gradually overtook the Minnatarees whose mounts were worn and tired from several days of travel on the warpath.

It was a hard ride, over jagged ridges, scrub-spattered

slopes, and dry washes in narrow, rock-strewn valleys.
The Minnatarees headed for the heavily timbered, rocky
shelf that jutted above the ground. The first to arrive
climbed to the place, dismounted, and found themselves in a natural fort, where they were well protected
by rocks and trees. As Holmes reports:

"They were at the wood; some had entered it and
leaped from their horses, and just as the last one was
within a few feet of it, Rose came within the reach of
his horse's tail. He seized it with his right hand and
gave his own horse a sudden turn to the left; both
horses and both men came to the ground in an instant,
and before either could recover the use of his legs or
weapons, a Crow had buried his club in the skull of
the Minnataree."

The rest of the Minnatarees were well protected.
The Crows knew how difficult it was to attack a place
so well defended and were not eager to make the attempt. The heat of revenge that had sent them on had
now cooled off. They were not eager to fight when there
was danger of loss.

But Cut Nose was not so easily discouraged. He was
made of different stuff. He remembered the Crow brave
who had been cut down from ambush without warning.

Turning to his hesitant companions, he told them,
"You are dogs that dare not bite until the wolf no
longer shows his teeth. You would run from a dead

badger. Follow me, and if you are afraid, let me hold your shields before you."

Few men would have dared to taunt Crow braves in such a fashion. But Ed Rose had spurred them and they now seemed willing to follow him to the stone battlements that protected the waiting Minnatarees.

Rose ran toward the natural fort that held the enemy. The Crow warriors followed, but their enthusiasm faded when five fell before a volley sent into their midst. They retreated, and Cut Nose stood on the breastworks, alone.

He paused for a breathless moment, a statue of courage. Then, slowly, he turned, disregarding danger. Contemptuously he walked back toward his warrior companions. Minnataree arrows fell harmlessly around him as he kept his measured pace.

The Crows had paused at a safe distance. Their hearts withered under his scornful gaze as he reached them. Deliberately he twanged his bow string, seeming to reach for words to describe the men who had deserted him.

"Squaws!" he said. The contempt in his voice was shattering. It was a fighting word. To a Crow warrior there was no greater insult than to be called a woman.

Ed Rose seized two shields, placed them together, and with nothing but his knife and battle axe, rushed forward to attack, alone. He was certain now that the

Crows would follow him. Now they would have to prove their manhood or suffer disgrace.

He reached the breastworks and leaped over the rocks. Two balls and three Minnataree arrows struck his double shield. Their force knocked him over. Holmes tells us, "His time, however, had not yet come, and, before the Minnatarees could turn around, he was in their den. He was a wolf in a sheep-fold. Such was their astonishment, that they could only stand and gaze."

The Crow warriors followed him this time. Cut Nose was alone and he was winning coups, honors that would be sung about and told about for years. His braves now rushed to share in the glory. Only the Minnataree boy, the moccasin carrier, escaped, and by good fortune reached his village safely.

When the battle was over, Edward Rose had a new name—Chee-ho-carte, or Five Scalps. The story of how he won his new name, the story of his bravery, would be told around camp fires for generations to come.

This exploit and other acts of bravery earned Ed Rose great honor among the Crows, and he became a chief in their tribe. His vigor, skill and intelligence were greatly admired by all members of the tribe.

Lieutenant Reuben Holmes was present when Rose was received by the Crows after a long absence. He tells us:

"Every child knew the exploit of that great brave, the 'Five Scalps'! The remembrance of it is still fresh among the Crows, and will so continue, as long as they exist as a nation. Their children are taught to lisp his name. . . . The whole village turned out to greet him. The old chiefs uttered an exclamation of surprise; the braves advanced and invited him to the feast. The young men, whom he had left as boys, crowded round him, and anxiously inquired if he had come to remain with them. . . . He had a word for everyone, and everyone a smile for him. . . . From the oldest to the youngest, there was, in fact, a genuine burst of joy at his arrival, and as genuine and a general expression of pleasure, at his intention to remain with them."

5

As a result of almost constant warfare, there were more women than men in the Indian tribes. The practice of men marrying more than one woman was common, but not every brave could support more than one wife, and good, hard-working squaws often had difficulty in finding husbands.

Rose became interested in an activity that involved escorting Arapaho squaws, who had been captured by the Snakes, to the Missouri River. Trappers there needed wives. They were engaged in a profitable trade and had the means to buy precious manufactured articles. They also made good husbands.

Lieutenant Holmes tells us that a man named Chabeneau engaged in this business with Rose. "Chabeneau" was probably Touissant Charbonneau, the husband of Sacajawea, an Indian, and one of the most remarkable women in American history. Charbonneau had gone to the Pacific with Lewis and Clark as an interpreter. Sacajawea had shared the hardships of the journey and more than once had saved the expedition.

As the two men and the six squaws they were escorting made ready to leave the Snake territory, Charbonneau was shocked to see Rose trade his gun for a quiver of arrows and a bow. The gun greatly exceeded the bow and arrows in value. It carried farther and was a much better weapon. But Rose was skilled in the use of a bow and arrow and could still bring down the necessary game on the trip.

For the next few days they made their way toward the Great Divide, the high point in the Rockies. Charbonneau continually criticized Cut Nose for his rashness in parting with his gun. While the Frenchman's harangue was continuing they met a small party of Snakes and Rose gave the bow and arrows to one of them, receiving nothing in return.

Such an act is not easy to explain or understand. It may have been simple generosity or it may have been Rose's way of showing his supreme self-confidence in the face of Charbonneau's fears.

Whatever the reason, Charbonneau was now desperate. He reproached Rose furiously. They were in wild country and they faced a long journey where either Indian enemies or starvation might appear. As Holmes tells the story, Charbonneau could not endure the idea of "dying on the wide prairie, without food and without water, with nothing but the damp grass for a bed, and the cold clouds floating in the blue heavens above him for a winding sheet."

Rose bore Charbonneau's new criticism for only a few moments. He called the Indian to whom he had given the bow and arrows. The man came and Ed gave him his knife.

Charbonneau was frantic. They had provisions for only one day, but Rose said to him, "The man who can't live in a country of game like this, without arms, deserves to die."

Rose's self-confidence was no comfort to his companion, but they moved on. We are not told how Charbonneau had lost his own gun, but in the whole party there was only one weapon of any kind—Charbonneau's knife.

For three days they saw no game and for two days ate not a mouthful of food. The squaws began to complain and Charbonneau was stricken with anguish. Finally, Rose asked to borrow his knife. When it was given to him, the Negro could not resist tantalizing poor Charbonneau still more. He broke the blade from its handle and laughed at Charbonneau's groan of despair, for the poor man was quite beyond speech.

They soon passed a willow thicket. Rose went into it and in a few minutes appeared with a willow sapling. The knife blade was attached to its tip. Armed with his new weapon, he went ahead of his party.

In midafternoon, as the sun was racing toward a

place beyond the rim of the mountains to the west, he came upon a huge brown beast. It was a buffalo. If the animal caught his scent it would be gone at a gallop and the life-saving meat would be lost.

With the stealth of an Indian, with the knowledge a man must have if he is to survive in a primitive world, Ed stalked the animal whose death and flesh meant life to eight famished people.

The time came. A final rush, a thrust, a roar, a frantic turn, and a dash to escape. But it was too late. Ed Rose stood over the dark, shaggy form as the sun dipped out of sight. A man, with a simple, handmade spear had done a hunter's work.

The squaws did a woman's work. They skinned the animal and jerked the meat, cutting it into thin strips and letting it dry in the sun. The jerked buffalo meat would make good meals for many days.

The rest of the trip was made with no incident other than the victories in the search for food by a man with a simple, primitive weapon and a superior hunter's skill.

6

EDWARD ROSE was to join almost every early expedition of importance to the Yellowstone country. The spring of 1809 found him with Ezekial Williams and a party of twenty men on the first all-land trip to the mountains.

Records of early western travel and exploration are not complete. Much of the information we have comes from letters and commercial records made by people who may or may not have had personal information of the event. In the case of the 1809 journey, our information comes from a book written by David H. Coyner, who worked from notes made by Ezekial Williams and from conversations with men engaged in the fur trade. Coyner's book bears the title, *The Lost Trappers,* and was published in 1859.

Coyner says that the Williams party escorted Big White back to the Mandans. Big White, or Sheheke, was the head chief of the Mandan Indians. He and his wife and child had accompanied Lewis and Clark to

Washington. It was extremely important that he be escorted safely back to his tribe. If he was not, if anything happened to him, it would cause serious trouble with the Mandans who occupied an important place on the Missouri, and who, if angered, could seriously affect river traffic.

Two trading parties and a military escort had attempted to return the chief to his home in 1807. A skirmish with the Aricaras and a band of Sioux forced them to return to St. Louis.

In 1809, the Missouri Fur Company was paid seven thousand dollars for the safe return of the Mandan chief. Lisa, Andrew Henry, William Clark, and other men experienced in the western fur trade were involved. The government could not afford to take any chances with the safety of Big White.

The expedition left St. Charles on June 15 and it is quite probable that Ezekial Williams was connected with the effort, though records of the time are rare and confused. Williams, Rose, and eighteen others left St. Louis in April. Each man was allotted a two years' supply of lead and powder and six beaver traps. The traps weighed five pounds each. Each man was also given an extra horse whose pack contained pistols, awls, axes, knives, camp kettles, blankets and "other essential little articles," as well as "little notions for presents" for the Indians. Four dogs accompanied them, including a greyhound which they expected to use for deer hunting.

We do not know the names of the eighteen other men, except that one was named William Hamilton and another Carson, though not Kit Carson, who first went west a dozen years later.

The twenty men followed the Missouri west to the Kansas River. By the twelfth day they were 240 miles from St. Louis. The dogs chased the wolves that surrounded their camp at night. At first the wolves ran away, as if afraid. The dogs were encouraged and followed, barking courageously. Then, suddenly, the wolves turned. The poor dogs found it was not a happy chase. Three of them, seriously hurt, managed to escape. The fourth was torn to pieces by the wild animals and scarcely a bone was to be found the next morning at the place.

On the fourteenth day their horses escaped. Fortunately, they were recovered. After that, the hobbles were fastened with the greatest possible care.

The small party crossed the Kansas River and went on a buffalo hunt with a village of Kansas Indians. They discovered that their horses were not suited for the sport. They had to be trained to run along the side of a buffalo to permit a good shot. The Indians' horses had learned to follow the running animals without guidance and drew close enough to give the rider a good aim.

Powerful Indian bows, made of wood or of bone and horn and lashed with rawhide could, in strong, expert hands, send an arrow through a buffalo. The Indians also used spears eight or ten feet long. They were pointed with sharp stone or a piece of metal. Iron and steel were more valuable than gold to the Indians.

The party moved north, keeping more than a hundred miles from the Missouri. By this means they avoided climbing up and down the bluffs near the river. They also kept clear of the widest and deepest parts of the tributary streams where they joined the Missouri and would be more difficult to cross.

Moving with forty horses, they lived in heat and storms and cold. They passed over unknown prairies, cut by ravines and gullies, crossed by creeks and rivers, each bearing its fair share of rocks, mud, and quicksand. They met strange Indian tribes, each of whom could include a score of braves, eager for a scalp. They moved through a country where law was made by each man and each man supplied his own defense.

While they might meet and even go hunting with Indians, they took no chances. They kept a sharp lookout in the daytime and moved with riders on each flank to prevent surprise in case of attack.

They stopped an hour before sundown, built a big fire, cooked and ate their supper while the horses refreshed themselves with prairie grass. After sunset they would quietly pack and move on eight or ten miles in the dark before stopping to spend the night in a fireless camp.

The night was split into four watches of three men each. They were on their way again before sunrise, following old buffalo trails, if one went in their direction. If not, they went over the plains and the rolling hills without marks or sign other than the sun and the stars.

Each day they killed game for food—antelope, deer, elk, buffalo, bear, prairie chickens, or wild water fowl. They crossed the Platte near the junction of the North and South Forks. Here, a Pawnee Indian admired one of their dogs. The dog was a mastiff and quite a different creature from the small, wolflike Indian dogs. They traded the dog for a buffalo horse. It was a good bargain all around and both parties were satisfied at the time. Unfortunately, the Indian came out a loser because two days later the dog caught up with the group. He had escaped his new Indian master.

The waving buffalo grass and the rolling hills made the men think of the ocean—an ocean on which not ships but giant herds of buffalo moved. Not hundreds, not thousands, but millions of buffalo. And the herds were followed by huge bands of wolves that got their dinner by separating a buffalo from the herd and worrying it and biting it until it fell from exhaustion and from its injuries.

There came a time when they heard a noise, the sound of thunder, on a clear day. They wondered what it could be. They were soon to know. It was buffalo, a stampede. A moving mass of animals that blackened the prairie swept down on them. They felt they would meet their end under the trampling hoofs. There seemed no way to escape.

Men and horses drew together. There was no place to run to avoid the huge brown force that was moving against them. Their only hope was to split the herd. So they made the best barricade they could of the baggage and did the only thing they could. They fired their guns into the advancing mass of wild fury. Some buffalo fell. Those following jumped over them or moved to one side. The men fired again, as fast as they could reload rifles and revolvers.

They shot and shouted. They waved hats and blankets. The stampeding herd crowded and pushed against each other. It was a tidal wave of bone and fur and muscle.

But when those in the lead began to turn aside, those that came after followed their leaders rather than face the shouting, shooting men. The herd split, and left them, a small island of safety in the midst of turmoil, dust, and thunder. Their only loss was one of the dogs, trampled to death while helping fight off the galloping animals.

7

THE travelers knew the trick of shooting antelope. No horse, no greyhound could outrun an antelope. The method of hunting them was to lie down in the deep prairie grass and carefully wave a stick with a bit of cloth tied to the end. The antelope would approach to see what this strange thing might be. When he got close enough a shot would bring him down. Curiosity killed the cat, they say. Curiosity also lured antelope to the hunters' cooking pots.

The men discovered that the Pawnee Indians treated their illnesses and bathed themselves by using steam baths. Hot rocks were placed in a small, tight enclosure made of branches and mud. Steam was produced by dashing water on the rocks. When the Indians were sufficiently steamed, they would plunge into a stream of cold water.

When one of their men sickened and died, they learned that a grave must be dug deep or covered with rocks or logs to keep the wolves away. In the wild chase of a buffalo hunt one of the horses was killed. It was late and they went back to camp expecting to return for the saddle. By the time they returned, they discovered that wolves ate not merely dead horses, but also their saddles.

The small party came upon many Indian villages, and Ed Rose served well as interpreter. When they approached the Sioux country they doubled all caution. They often traveled at night and, when possible, in ravines or gullies to keep out of sight and avoid an ambush. There were many Sioux bands between the Platte, the Black Hills, and the Mandan villages on the Missouri, and the Sioux were known as land pirates. Every effort was made to avoid the Sioux.

The goods Ed Rose and his party possessed represented indescribable wealth to Indians. The value of a steel knife, an axe, or an awl to a man who had only crude instruments made of stone or bone can hardly be imagined. To an Indian squaw a cooking pot was of value far beyond measure.

Ed Rose and brave men like him moved freely and at ease when they traveled alone without such riches. But they maintained their position and personal property by sheer courage and the ability to stand off any Indian who might step forth.

On July 1, after almost three months of hard travel, the party reached the Mandan villages. Big White was delivered to his tribe safe and sound. They took a few

days to rest and then moved toward the headwaters of
the Missouri to search for good beaver streams. It was
near Blackfoot country. Here all dangers were mul-
tiplied. Washington Irving wrote that it was ". . . country over which roves and prowls the ferocious Blackfeet Indians, then as well as now one of the most cruel
and relentless tribes of the far west. For the Black-feet
Indian is an embodiment of every quality that is offen-
sive to the feelings of civilized man."

At the Yellowstone they turned southwest and followed the river toward the Big Horn. Here, they
trapped and rested. Their horses, too, needed time to
recover from their hard, long trip over the Bad Lands.
They needed time for sore backs and sore feet to mend,
time for lush prairie grass to put a layer of fat on gaunt
loins and over the ridges of sharp ribs stretching against
galled, sweat-stained hide.

Fish and game were plenty. But it was not to be a
peaceful, restful time. Ten men hunting buffalo were
attacked by Blackfeet. Only five escaped. The trappers
were certain they were being watched. They knew they
could expect another attack. Their only question was
when the attack would come.

Coyner's book tells us: "When night came on, all
hands were busy collecting their traps and making
ready for their departure that night as soon as possible."
They built large fires to deceive the enemy, and cau-
tiously withdrew a mile. "About midnight they leaped

into their saddles and set out south. They travelled as fast as they could for twenty four hours, without giving repose to themselves or horses."

They soon reached the Crows. Ed Rose, an old friend of the Crows, and a chief among them, was a good man to be with. He was in the land where he was known as Chee-ho-carte, Five Scalps. The Crows received them as friends. They remained a week, then moved south toward the sources of the Platte River. Here, the Crows pointed out the route. Rose "expressed his intention to abandon his party and remain among the Crows."

Edward Rose was home again. Home, in Absaroka, the land of the Crows.

8

In the summer of 1811, the largest party the fur business on the western rivers had seen or would see for more than ten years paused before the Aricara villages on the Missouri River. And as if on cue in a drama, a heavily muscled Negro in Indian clothing appeared, riding alone down the prairie hills and across the river bottom. It was Edward Rose.

We do not know precisely where Rose had been since his journey to Absaroka two years before with Ezekial Williams, but it can be assumed he was with the Crows. We do not know how the news reached him that a new party was ascending the river, but we do know that he made his appearance on a June day in 1811, and that he was engaged as a guide and interpreter.

The party he met was led by Wilson Price Hunt, a partner of John Jacob Astor, one of the country's most famous and richest fur merchants. Astor had been born in Germany in 1763. At the age of sixteen he went to

London and for a few years worked for his brother who manufactured and sold musical instruments. In November, 1783, with his small capital invested in musical instruments, he sailed for America. Two months later, his ship was in Chesapeake Bay and was firmly locked in ice. The thaws did not come until March and it was then that he set his feet down in Baltimore.

He didn't know it during the weeks he chafed impatiently at the delay of the icebound ship, but the time was well spent. He had fallen in with a dealer of furs from whom he received advice and information about the fur trade. With the proceeds of the sale of his musical instruments he entered the fur business and made rapid progress.

By 1800, Astor was a leading fur merchant. He had done well, but he was not through. The Louisiana Purchase opened new horizons to those who could see them, and Astor had the vision. In 1808, he created the American Fur Company. His plan was to gather furs in the Far West. It would require an investment of $400,000. It would also require a great many associates and employees.

A ship was to go around South America to the mouth of the Columbia River on the northwestern coast. At the same time a party was to go by land, over the route of Lewis and Clark. They were to meet, and establish a post on the Pacific at Astoria, to draw on and to serve the fur rich country. The ship was the *Tonquin.* She

was completely staffed and loaded for the fur trade and
she put Sandy Hook, the mouth of New York's harbor,
behind her on September 8, 1810.

The overland party, known as the Astorians, was to
be led by Wilson Price Hunt, a merchant from New
Jersey who had been engaged in the fur trade in St.
Louis since 1804. He had never been in the field as a
hunter or trapper and was thus not very well equipped
to head such an expedition. Other partners who were
to make the journey were much more experienced in
travel in the wilderness.

Donald McKenzie, a partner, started with Hunt from
New York in June of 1810 to go to St. Louis by way
of Montreal, the Ottawa River, Lake Michigan, the
Fox, Wisconsin, and Mississippi rivers. They enlisted
hunters and boatmen called *voyageurs* in Canada. They
also engaged more men in St. Louis where they arrived
on September 3. Joseph Miller, a former Army officer
who had become a trapper, was accepted as a partner.

They passed the winter at the mouth of the Nodawa
River, now called the Nodaway, near the present site
of St. Joseph, Missouri. Although the rivers were frozen
over, preparations for the long journey continued. It
was to be the first expedition to the Pacific since the
journey by Meriwether Lewis and William Clark half
a dozen years before.

The other partners arrived—Robert McLellan who

had been in the Indian wars in Ohio, an excellent woodsman, and Ramsay Crooks, a Scotsman who had been in the fur trade in Canada. McLellan and Crooks had been partners in the fur trade with the Omaha Indians, above the mouth of the Platte.

Pierre Dorion was engaged as an interpreter. He was the son of the Dorion who had acted as interpreter for Lewis and Clark and had been up the river with Manuel Lisa the year before. His wife, a Sioux squaw, and their two small children were with him.

In April, 1811, the party broke camp and moved against the flood waters of the Missouri. They had four boats and carried three small cannon. The five partners were accompanied by the interpreter and his family, a clerk, forty Canadian *voyageurs,* and several hunters and trappers.

Manuel Lisa, leading a trapping expedition, also left St. Louis in April with twenty men and caught up with the Astorians below the villages of the Aricaras. The combined parties faced the dangerous Aricara Indians with a feeling of confidence. Their ranks were torn, however, with jealousy and strife. Lisa and Dorion nursed a mutual grudge arising out of a conflict the year before. McLellan and Crooks held an enmity against Lisa which sprang from old rivalries. Hunt was afraid Lisa might incite the Aricaras against him. These hatreds and the fears they bred were never far from

flaming into gunfire and bloodshed, but the greater
danger of the treacherous Aricaras forced an uneasy
peace.

Hunt had planned to continue up the river, but news
reached him that the dangers presented by the Mandans, Sioux, and Blackfeet Indians were too great. So
he considered leaving the river and taking an unknown
march overland to the mountain passes.

The party had three guides, none of whom had been
west of the eastern slope of the Rocky Mountains. The
presence of the savage Aricaras, the knowledge of still
more savage tribes to come, stories of the hardship of
land travel, of thirst and hunger, caused the Canadians
to talk of desertion. But they were foiled in their attempt to steal boats and arms and return to St. Louis.

It was at this time Rose appeared. We may be sure
that his old friend Lisa greeted him with a howl of joy
and that Dorion also roared a greeting. Very probably
so did McLellan and Crooks who had traded with the
Omahas and who undoubtedly knew the big Negro.

Here was a man Hunt needed. The Astorians were
well financed. They carried a treasure of manufactured
goods, and needed all the help they could get. In Indian
eyes, Hunt's party possessed goods of greater value than
gold.

Edward Rose was the answer to Hunt's greatest need.
The dark-skinned man knew the Crow and other Indian languages. The land route would take them

through Absaroka, the home of the Crows, where Rose was respected and admired. Indeed, he held a high position in their councils. Rose knew the route, and with him, Hunt could leave the river and avoid the Mandans, Sioux, and Blackfeet. Or, if marauding war parties could not be avoided, a man with Rose's experience and knowledge would be an ideal one to have.

The Astorians could not get all the horses they wanted from the Aricaras, but they traded their boats to Lisa and other goods with the Indians, and on July 18, 1811, set off over unmarked prairies. Lisa would remain and trap along the tributaries of the Missouri.

Hiram Martin Chittenden, in *A History of the American Fur Trade in the Far West,* reports this historic event:

"Hunt with his whole party took up their long and uncertain journey to the westward. It was a serious moment to most of them, for no one knew what lay ahead, and they found little consolation in the doubtful looks of Lisa's people who had been on the upper rivers."

Washington Irving, in his book *Astoria,* a history of the activities of the American Fur Company in attempting to establish the Pacific Coast fur trade, gives expression to similar forebodings:

"The veteran trappers and voyageurs of Lisa's party shook their heads as their comrades set out, and took leave of them as of doomed men; and even Lisa himself gave it as his opinion, after the travelers had departed, that they would never reach the shores of the Pacific, but would either perish with hunger in the wilderness, or be cut off by the savages."

Whatever other men may have thought, there was one man who faced the setting sun with confidence. Ed Rose had gone to the western mountains at least twice before this.

There were sixty-four people, including Dorion's squaw and the two children. They traveled with eighty-four horses. The Indian woman walked with the men. She would endure the same hardships as they. Seventy-six of the horses were laden with baggage, traps, amunition, bedding, corn meal, Indian trade goods, and other necessaries. One horse was for Dorion's baggage and his two children, and each of the five partners rode. The guides and hunters, eyes sharp, guns in hand, moved ahead and on the flanks, always on the lookout for game or Indians.

With the guides, and usually at the head of the long train, was the man on whom the safety of the journey to the land of the Crows depended. He was a muscular black man, with a cut nose and a thick scar on his forehead, Edward Rose.

9

Hunt's route took him over immense prairies, bare of trees. In the heat of the summer days the sun burned against a hard blue sky. In the coolness of the nights the stars sparkled with brittle brilliance and seemed close enough to be within reach of a shot from a buffalo gun.

Kettles were distributed and the camp was divided into small messes. There were tents for the partners, but everyone else slept in the open where they could look up at the stars as they closed their eyes in sleep, or where they found no sleep at all when rain clouds smothered the stars and lightning filled the plains with blazing streaks of fire.

After five days of travel they stopped on the banks of the Grand River, near the camp of a band of Cheyenne Indians. The two parties spent a pleasant two weeks exchanging gifts and visits. The Cheyennes were well-behaved people, clean, vigorous, and well dressed in garments beautifully made of hides and furs. They were excellent horsemen and Hunt bought thirty-six horses from them.

Horses were given to Ed Rose and five others. The rest of the animals were distributed among the *voyageurs,* who took turns riding. They were now far enough from the Missouri so that Hunt began to feel easy about the men. He was no longer afraid of their desertion. There was safety in the large group and not many men would have the courage to face the dangers of the prairie alone.

But Wilson Price Hunt acquired a new fear, an unreasoned fear of Edward Rose. Someone in the party told Hunt that Rose was secretly trying to encourage the men to revolt when they reached the Crows, and make away with whatever goods and horses they wanted. Instead of bringing the matter into the open and getting at the truth, Hunt told his partners quietly. They, too, kept the rumor secret and lived in fear and watchfulness. In so doing, Hunt denied Rose the opportunity to confront his accuser.

Rose's cut nose and the fierce scar on his forehead did not inspire Hunt's confidence. Hunt was in surroundings that were strange to him. He bore a great responsibility as he was the master of an expedition that represented a tremendous investment. It may be that his rejection of Rose was a fundamental cause of his later difficulties and failure. If he had kept the black man in his service, Rose, with his skill and knowledge of the western mountains probably would have been able to bring the expedition success. Hunt's fears were as unfounded and as unsubstantial as had been his fears of Lisa as he approached the Aricaras.

Constance L. Skinner, in *Adventurers of Oregon,* says that "Hunt's ignorance of wilderness life came near to wrecking the overland expedition." And she points out that Hunt failed to enlist the crew he needed. If Hunt had only known it, he had in Rose exactly the man who could guide him safely to his destination. But for some reason, Hunt could not bring himself to trust the Negro mountain man.

The mature judgment of history is that Hunt had nothing at all to fear from Rose. In *The American Fur Trade in the Far West,* Chittenden says:

"Certain suspicious actions of Rose had induced the belief that he was plotting to betray the party to the Crows. How far these suspicions were well founded cannot be said, but the probabilities are all against them. At any rate, Hunt was badly worked up over the matter and resorted to precautions which seem almost ridiculous, considering the strength of his party."

Mr. Hunt's foolish fears led him to go so far as to promise a reward to Rose upon passing safely through Crow country. He offered half a year's wages, a horse, and three beaver traps. It is difficult to imagine how Hunt could have thought such a paltry reward would have influenced Rose. If Rose had any unlawful intentions he would have been most unlikely to let the vast wealth of more than a hundred horses and tons of precious merchandise slip away from him for such a modest payment.

The party snaked its way in a slender line along the Grand River, north of the Black Hills of South Dakota. They left the prairie and moved over steep rocky ridges and deep valleys. Their trail took them beneath savage cliffs which towered above them in fantastic forms. They climbed wild jungles of rocks, envious of the bighorn sheep that watched them with wide-eyed curiosity for a moment before springing lightly away on the rims of dizzy precipices.

When the hills faded and the land opened out into prairie, buffalo herds gave them good eating and travel was easier.

The uplands, between the creekbeds, led them over rough buttes and through broken gullies. Barren, arid hills where there was no game brought hunger and still more fatigue. The hot summer sun dried the small creeks. Showers or torrents of rain were devoured by the parched earth and left only a steaming heat.

At one time they had twenty-five miles of painful travel without a drop of water. Again, they had a stretch of eighteen scorching, bone-dry miles, and one dreadful day of parched throats and swollen tongues, of heat and toil. Mr. McKenzie's dog died of thirst.

On the rock-strewn heights of land game was scarce

and wolf meat was all they had. But still they moved through the Bad Lands. The weary miles passed beneath their feet and slowly a dim, blue ridge on the western horizon rose higher and higher. As the long days wore away they moved toward the Big Horn range and Absaroka, the land of the Crows.

They crossed the Little Missouri, the Little Powder, and the Powder River. Here, they saw ". . . to their great joy once more wide grassy meadows, stocked with herds of buffalo . . . the buffaloes were in such abundance that they were enabled to kill as many as they pleased, and jerk a sufficient supply of meat for several days journeying."

On August 22, tracks in the rough soil showed that a large party of Indians had passed that way. The partners and *voyageurs* paused in silence and alarm. Ed Rose examined the tracks carefully. The shape of footprints left by moccasin soles were full of meaning to a man who knew the signs. Kidney-shaped tracks with a deep instep distinguished Crow prints from the more triangular or oval prints of Sioux, Cheyenne, Arapaho, Blackfeet, or Pawnee.

Were these tracks made by Blackfeet? Sioux? No. Ed gave a sign. They were Crows. Though Mr. Hunt feared Rose, he had to trust him to read the footprints. Too bad he didn't trust him completely. His expedition might have had a much happier conclusion.

The party moved on. By August 30, they were four hundred miles from the Missouri and the Aricara villages. Four hundred miles had been covered in forty-two days.

10

THEY were now in the land of the Crows, who tended to be more friendly than many of the other tribes. It was country Ed Rose knew, and he was held in respect by the Crow Indians. But hunters or raiding parties from neighboring tribes might be anywhere. It was not possible that the expedition would not be seen.

Two mounted figures appeared in the distance. Washington Irving describes the moment:

". . . in the edge of the evening, not long after they had encamped at the foot of the Big Horn Sierra, a couple of wild-looking beings, scantily clad in skins, but well armed, and mounted on horses as wild-looking as themselves, were seen approaching with great caution from among the rocks. They might have been mistaken for two of the evil spirits of the mountains so formidable in Indian fable."

Savages who might have been taken for evil spirits! If the suspicious Wilson Price Hunt knew of such beliefs, his heart must have stopped for a long moment.

But no matter how afraid or excited he may have been, he now pushed aside his doubts of Edward Rose's loyalty and called on the black man for help.

It was a tense moment of obvious danger. Rose mounted and rode toward the two strange Indians. Was it a trap? Who knew if there were only two? How many other Indians were hiding back of the rocks, ready to attack? It could be a raiding party of Blackfeet, Sioux, Cheyennes.

If Rose felt fear he did not show it. Sixty men stayed behind. Ed Rose advanced and faced whatever danger there was to face, alone.

He approached the two Indians. There was a moment's parley. Then three men rode together toward the Astorians. The Indians were Crows. They accepted the dark man with the scarred face as a friend.

Now, the safety of Hunt's party depended entirely on Ed Rose. There were thousands of Crow warriors in Absaroka, and Rose was a Crow chief. If he chose, the Astorians would disappear before the Crows like a gopher in the paws of a grizzly bear. But he did not choose betrayal.

The next day a large band of Crow warriors swept toward the camp, hoofbeats thundering on the prairie sod, whoops and yells splitting the air, and, we may be sure, making Wilson Price Hunt's spine chill. But it was only show, a show of pleasure at the return of their chief, Chee-ho-carte—Five Scalps.

Big White, also known as Sheheke or Shahaka, who was escorted back to his Mandan village on the Missouri by a party that included Edward Rose. He rendered friendly services to Lewis and Clark and had accompanied them to Washington where he was given a medal. From a portrait by St. Menin, 1805.

Wilson Price
Hunt

Manuel Lisa

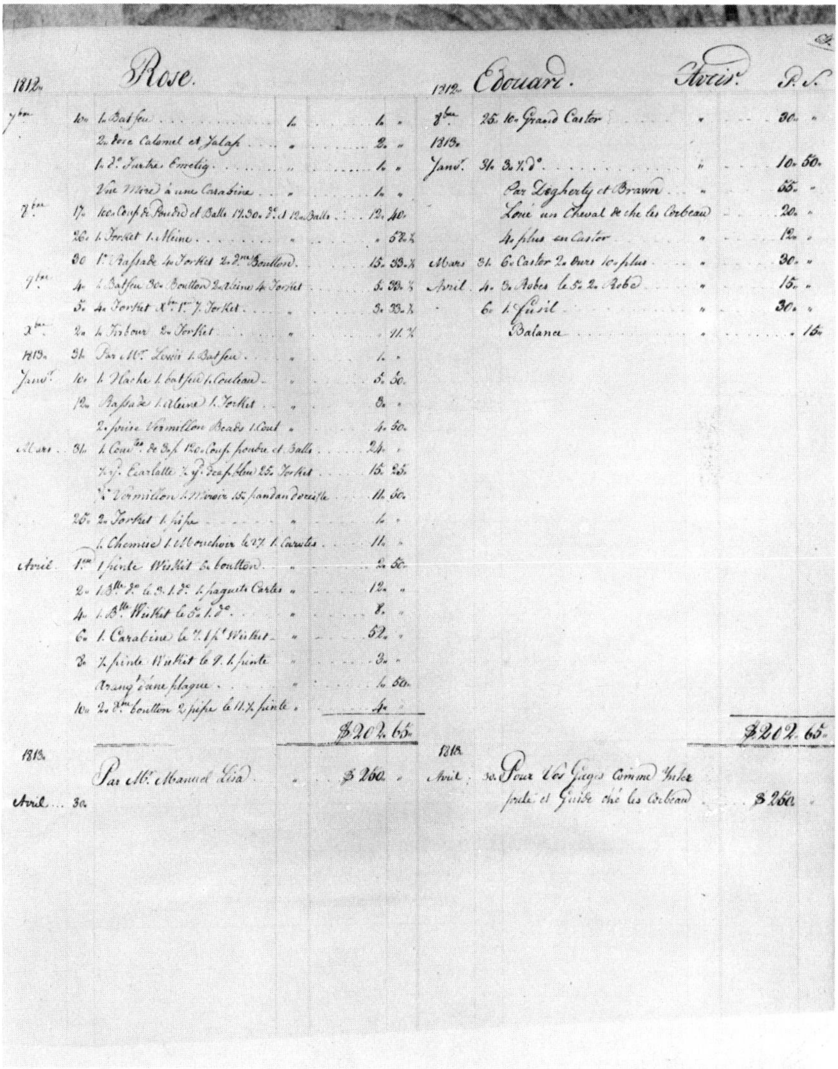

1812		Rose.		
7bre	10	1 Batfeu	1	1
		2 dose Calomel et Jalap		2
		1 d° Tartre Emetiq		1
		Une Mire à une Carabine		1
7bre	17	100 Coup de Poudre et Balle 17.30 d° 12 Balle		12 40
	26	1 Torket 1 Aleine		52½
	30	1 Rassade 4 Torket 2 d.mes Boullon		15 33½
9bre	4	1 Batfeu 30 Boullon 2 Aleine 4 Torket		5 33½
	5	4 Torket Xbre 1er 7 Torket		3 33½
Xbre	2	1 Tirbour 2 Torket		11½
1813	31	Par Mr Lewis 1 Batfeu		1
Janvr	10	1 Hache 1 batfeu 1 Couteau		5 50
	12	Rassade 1 Aleine 1 Torket		3
		2 paire Vermillon Beads 1 Cout		4 50
Mars	31	1 Couvte de 3 p 120 Coup poudre et Balle		24
		½ v. Ecarlatte ½ v. Drap bleu 25 Torket		15 25
		½ Vermillon 1 Miroir 15 pandan d'oreille		11 50
	25	2 Torket 1 pipe		1
		1 Chemise 1 Mouchoir à 7 1 Carotes		11
Avril	1er	1 pinte Wiskey 6 boullon		2 50
	2	1 Blle d° à 3 1 d° 1 paquet Cartes		12
	4	1 Blle Wiskey à 5 1 d°		8
	6	1 Carabine à 7 1 pt Wiskey		52
	8	½ pinte Wiskey à 9 1 pinte		3
		Arrang d'une plaque		1 50
	10	2 d.mes boullon 2 pipe à 11½ pinte		4
				$202 65
1813		Par Mr Manuel Lisa		$260
Avril	30			

1812		Edouard.	Avoir	P. S.
8bre	25	10 Grand Castor		30
1813				
Janvr	31	3½ d°		10 50
		Par Dogherty et Brawn		55
		Loué un Cheval de che les Corbeau		20
		4 plus en Castor		12
Mars	31	6 Castor 2 Ours 10 plus		30
Avril	4	3 Robes à 5 2 Robe		15
	6	1 Fusil		30
		Balance		15
				$202 65
1818				
Avril	30	Pour Vos Gages Comme Interprete et Guide ché les Corbeau		$260

The Kansas State Historical Society

Account page with the Missouri Fur Company for Edward Rose

"Prairie Picnic Disturbed by Rushing Herd of Buffalo," by George Catlin

Joslyn Art Museum, Omaha, Nebraska

"Bison-Dance of the Mandan Indians," by Charles Bodmer

"A Blackfoot Indian on Horseback," by Charles Bodmer

"Taking a Hump Rib," by Alfred Jacob Miller

"Beaver Hut on the Missouri," by Charles Bodmer

"Trapper's Encampment," by Alfred Jacob Miller

"Bull Boating on the Platte River," by Alfred Jacob Miller

"Trappers," by Alfred Jacob Miller

"Indian Lodge" (interior), by Alfred Jacob Miller

"Pawnee Indians Migrating," by Alfred Jacob Miller

"Approaching Buffalo," by Alfred Jacob Miller

"Killing Buffalo with the Lance," by Alfred Jacob Miller

"Indians on the War Path," by Alfred Jacob Miller

"Prairie on Fire," by Alfred Jacob Miller

"Capture of Wild Horses by Indians," by Alfred Jacob Miller

"Winter Village of the Minatarres," by Charles Bodmer

"View of the Rocky Mountains," by Charles Bodmer

"Indian Council," by Alfred Jacob Miller

"Indian Boy," by George Catlin

After the boisterous welcome, the two parties rode sixteen miles to the Crow camp where the easterners were received as guests and made welcome. Mr. Hunt gave the Crows presents—a scarlet blanket to one of the chiefs, to others some powder and balls, knives, awls, tobacco, and trinkets.

The Indians, in turn, gave gifts to their guests. The following day was passed in trading. Exhausted horses and trade goods were exchanged for fresh mounts, skins, and robes. The Crows had thousands of horses and before the trading was over the Astorians had 121 sound, active horses, well suited for mountain service.

Edward Rose was a man who showed little humor or pleasure and this, to some extent, may have given him the reputation for being sullen and for having a sinister look. The cut nose and the deep scar were severe handicaps and must have made him appear a forbidding and dangerous man. But the white men were now on his home grounds. He was a genial host and moved through the encampment making sure that things went smoothly and that no trouble occurred.

Even now it seemed not to have occurred to Hunt that the promise of a horse, three traps, and half a year's salary was meaningless to Rose. As a Crow chief, he possessed hundreds of horses. He had no need for three traps, as he knew how to make Indian traps, snares, and deadfalls, which he could use to catch all the animals he wanted. Buffalo for hides and meat covered the prairies

of Absaroka. And Rose had no real need for half a
year's pay. A hundred and fifty dollars in money had
no meaning to one in his position. He could trade hides
and furs for everything he needed or wanted.

It seems strange that the other partners offered no
objection to Hunt's unreasoned fears. Perhaps he
would not have listened if they had, so convinced was
he that the one whispered rumor was to be believed.
Certainly nothing Rose had done justified anything
but admiration and confidence. And there was to be
still further evidence of Rose's good will toward the
Astorians.

11

Rose had performed his duty. He had led Hunt's party to Absaroka as he had agreed to do. He was content to remain with the Crows. Good-byes were said and Hunt continued on his way with a sense of relief. He followed along the side of the mountain range, looking for a way to turn to the west and cross over it, another step toward the far Pacific.

In fifteen miles of travel he found no pass. The mountains towered above the party of Astorians and they could find no way to get through. The next day, September 3, they had no more luck. The mountains still barred their way.

They tried to force a passage over the range, but became lost among the rocks. They worked themselves away from the water courses. Their thirst became painful. Many of the men wandered off in search of a spring.

Again and again they tried to find a pass. Again and again they failed. Hunt withdrew six miles to a stream and built a signal fire to guide the lost men back to camp.

Wilson Price Hunt was at his wit's end. All the guides, the interpreters, and the partners could find no way to cross the mountain range. They were exhausted. It had been another day of painful and fruitless scrambling.

The next morning Ed Rose appeared with a band of Crows. Mr. Hunt's heart may have again thumped with fear, but Rose still showed no sign of treachery. On the contrary, he invited the Astorians to join him. Whatever misgivings Mr. Hunt may have had, he accepted the offer of aid, and the two cavalcades of white men and red men, led by a black man, wound in long lines through the rugged defiles, up and down the steeps of the mountains.

The mountain trail was rough and broken and the parties followed Ed as his horse moved between the rocks and along the ledges, through passages that seemed to have no exit. Then, suddenly, it was over. The way was clear. They were across the mountains that had stopped them, the forbidding peaks that had seemed to contain no pass.

Rose and the Crow Indians drew aside and the Astorians streamed past. Ed sat on his mount, a picture of confidence, strength, and skill. He waved the easterners on.

Men such as Edward Rose, the very early mountain

men and trappers, were the links between the two cultures, Indian and white, that were meeting for the first
time. Sydney Greenbie, in *Furs to Furrows,* says:

"Edward Rose, the white-black-red man, was of such
as these. Unfortunately for Hunt, they were too suspicious of him to take his advice in the conduct of the
trip. Rose played them fair, and the party passed safely
through the Crow country, and left him behind to play
hero to later tales."

Mr. Hunt may have breathed a sigh of relief, but he
should have left Rose reluctantly. The Astorians later
lost their way and suffered sad misadventure when the
advice and guidance of an experienced mountain man
such as Edward Rose could have prevented it.

Hunt made a mistake which led to disaster. He
abandoned his horses and built canoes to navigate the
Snake River. It couldn't be done successfully. With the
party broken up, the small groups suffered agonizing
hardship. Hunger, sickness, death came to them. Some
of the men finally arrived at Astoria, but the expedition
was a failure—a failure that became its certain fate
within a few days after Edward Rose left the group.

It is unfortunate that many people form their opinions of others because of their appearance, and it is possible that Hunt was persuaded to mistrust Rose because
of his unfortunate scar and grotesque nose. Mr. Hunt
was unable to look beneath Edward Rose's black,
scarred face and see the man within.

12

FOR the next decade a curtain is drawn over details of Edward Rose's life. Historians agree that he spent most of that time with the Crows, winning still more recognition in the tribe. It is believed that he also spent three years with the Aricaras.

A great movement to the fur country was under way. William H. Ashley and Andrew Henry were partners in the Rocky Mountain Fur Company and they began to organize large expeditions of trappers for the Rocky Mountain fur trade. As he had done before, and as he would do again, Ed Rose showed up and got a job. An old-timer, he had knowledge, skills, experience, and fierce energy that were very much in demand.

Ashley was overjoyed to hire Rose when he rode into the trappers' camp south of the Aricara villages in 1823. Here was a man who had worked for Henry over a dozen years before. He had also worked for Lisa and for Hunt. He knew a dozen Indian tongues and the Indian sign language. He had been a chief of the Crows for almost a decade and had spent several years with the Aricaras. He was strong, he knew the prairies and mountains, he was a crack shot. Brave beyond the telling, he would often go as far to get into a scrap as most men would to get out of one. Ed Rose was a first-rate man to have on the dangerous trip to the mountains. None better. Little wonder that Ashley was quick to hire him.

Ashley had left St. Louis on March 10, 1823, with a hundred men. They traveled in two keelboats and the Rocky Mountains were their goal. They were in search of beaver. Ashley and Henry had led an expedition of a hundred men the year before. Bad luck had plagued them, but Henry, with some of the men, had reached their destination and had remained on the Yellowstone. Ashley had returned to St. Louis and now was again going up the river.

Ashley, born in Virginia in 1778, had gone to St. Louis in 1802. There he engaged in the real estate business, the manufacture of gunpowder, in mining, and banking. In 1820, he was elected the first Lieutenant Governor of Missouri. He was active in the Missouri militia and had risen in the ranks until he became a general in 1822. Later—from 1831 to 1837—he served as congressman from Missouri.

Andrew Henry came from Fayette County, Pennsylvania. The exact date of his birth, sometime between 1773 and 1778, is not known. Nor is it known when he

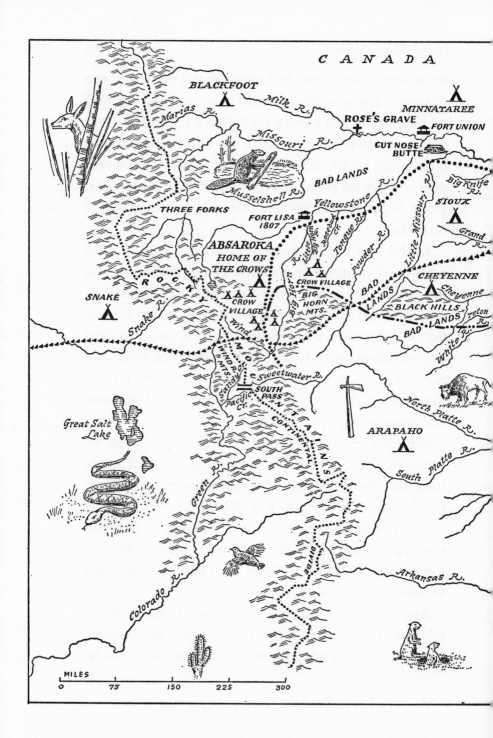

CANADA

BLACKFOOT

Marias R.

Milk R.

Missouri R.

ROSE'S GRAVE

MINNATAREE

FORT UNION

CUT NOSE BUTTE

Musselshell R.

BAD LANDS

Big Knife R.

THREE FORKS

Yellowstone R.

Torque R.

SIOUX

Grand R.

FORT LISA 1807

Little Horn R.

Rosebud Ck.

Powder R.

Little Missouri R.

ABSAROKA
HOME OF
THE CROWS

256 1yo.

CROW VILLAGE

CHEYENNE

Cheyenne

SNAKE

R O C K Y

CROW
VILLAGE

Snake R.

BIG
HORN
MTS.

Big Horn R.

BAD
LANDS

BLACK HILLS

BAD LANDS

Teton R.

Wind R.

WINDROS MTS.

Sandy Ck.

Sweetwater R.

White R.

MOUNTAINS

Pacific Ck.

SOUTH
PASS

CONTINENTAL

North Platte R.

Great Salt
Lake

ARAPAHO

DIVIDE

South Platte R.

Green R.

Colorado R.

Arkansas R.

MILES

0   75   150   225   300

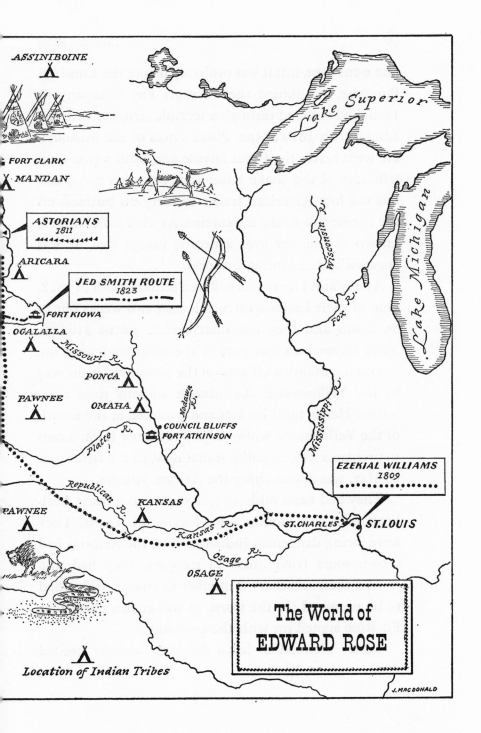

ASSINIBOINE

FORT CLARK
MANDAN

ASTORIANS
1811

ARICARA

JED SMITH ROUTE
1823

FORT KIOWA

OGALALLA

Missouri R.

PONCA

PAWNEE

OMAHA

COUNCIL BLUFFS
FORT ATKINSON

Nodawa R.

Platte R.

EZEKIAL WILLIAMS
1809

Republican R.

KANSAS

PAWNEE

Kansas R.

ST. CHARLES ST. LOUIS

Osage R.

OSAGE

Lake Superior

Wisconsin R.

Fox R.

Lake Michigan

Mississippi R.

The World of
EDWARD ROSE

Location of Indian Tribes

J. MAC DONALD

first went west, but it was probably before the Lousiana
Purchase. He joined the Missouri Fur Company in
1809, and suffered through a terrible struggle with the
Blackfeet in 1810 at the Three Forks of the Missouri.
He went across the Great Divide and built a post on a
tributary of the Snake River that bears his name and
was the first American trader to carry on business on
the Pacific side of the mountains. As with Rose, little is
known of him for over a decade except that he was
engaged in the mining business.

Ashley and Henry had suffered serious losses in 1822.
One of their keelboats struck a snag two weeks out of
St. Louis and they lost merchandise worth $10,000.
They rescued a small part of the cargo and went on.
Above the Mandan villages on the Missouri, on the way
to the Yellowstone, Assiniboine Indians stole their
horses. Henry built his fort and wintered at the mouth
of the Yellowstone while Ashley returned to St. Louis
to prepare a new expedition that now, in the latter part
of May, was approaching the Aricara villages.

They had been pushing and pulling the heavy keelboats over two months since leaving St. Louis. They
were facing dangerous Indians. While the Aricaras had
shown some friendliness to trappers, they had also
proved their treachery a number of times. Ashley had
to be prepared for the worst. It was at this point that
Ed Rose signed on with the company.

Ashley planned to leave the river and he needed

horses for the land journey to the mountains. He opened trade with the Indians. At the invitation of an Aricara chief, he visited the village with Rose and was quite thrown off guard by expressions of friendship. But Edward Rose was not deceived. He cautioned Ashley that trouble of some sort was brewing. But Ashley ignored his advice. His forces were poorly distributed, a fact which Rose recognized. His men were split in two groups. Forty men were on a sand bar extending out into the river, near the Indian village, while the boats were anchored dangerously close to shore with the rest of the men aboard. As Chittenden tells us:

"Ashley seems to have been about as suspicious of Rose as Hunt had been twelve years before, and with just as little reason. He rejected Rose's advice to moor the boats for the night against a bar on the opposite side of the river and not only remained near the shore next to the villages, but even left his land party. . . . The party numbered about forty men, and had with them all the horses which had been purchased."

A man in Ashley's position, dealing with Indians whose language he did not understand, had one paramount need. That was for an interpreter. Skill and honesty in an interpreter are basic. We cannot know why General Ashley made Hunt's error, though it was a mistake many employers make. He hired a good man and then failed to accept his employee's opinion in the field of his unique talent. And Ed Rose was more than an interpreter. He had a rare knowledge of Indian ways and character. But the forty men on the bar, and the horses, were left in jeopardy.

Early the following morning the Aricaras killed one of Ashley's men and threatened immediate attack. At daylight, the favorite time for Indians to attack, they began firing on the small party camped on the sand bar. But before the shooting started, the Aricaras called to Rose and told him to leave the trappers and save himself. This he refused to do.

The fire was intense. The boatmen, in a panic, refused to move the keelboats closer to shore to take aboard the forty men who were under fire.

Some of the men on the beach felt the situation was hopeless. They retreated into the river and swam for the boats. Ashley sent two skiffs ashore which were big enough to rescue thirty men. But most of the land party, Rose among them, determined not to retreat. Only seven men, four of whom were wounded, took to the boats.

The sharp crack of rifle fire continued to echo across the Missouri until all of the horses were either killed or had broken their tethers and had run away. Half of the men on the bar were either killed or wounded.

More men retreated. Ed Rose and Hugh Glass, two of the old-timers, covered the retreat. At last Hugh, too, plunged into the stream and swam under water as long as he could, and continued amid a shower of balls and arrows.

Rose covered Glass' swim to safety, but one rifle could not hold the Aricaras back any longer. The savages were leaving their shelter and running toward him.

It was late, almost too late. Ed Rose ran to the water and swam for the boat. Those watching wondered at the courage of the man who had remained so long on the shore. They watched in amazement as his strong strokes sped him through the muddy water and as bullets and arrows splashed around him.

Lieutenant Reuben Holmes, in *The Five Scalps,* describes Rose's activity in the battle and says of him that he had ". . . at the very commencement, taken his station behind a small bunch of willows, from which, detached and alone, he fired as often as an Indian showed himself. . . . He apparently thought of nothing but the work in which he was engaged; all ideas of boats and safety had fled before the excitement of a scene so congenial to his feeling; nor was it, until he had been repeatedly called by . . . General Ashley . . . that he raised himself from the posture he had, Indian-like, assumed, and looked around him; he then saw, in himself, the sole occupant of the bar . . . the Indians rushing from the village to take the scalps of those killed. . . . He plunged into the stream and swam for the boats, amid the pattering of a shower of balls on the water around him; he reached one of them, rifle in hand, in safety, and was the last man to do so."

The conflict had raged fiercely. It was all over in less than half an hour. When Glass and Rose reached the boats, the anchor of one was raised, the cable of the other was cut, and they floated downstream out of reach of the Indians' fire.

Ed Rose and Hugh Glass stood beside each other puffing hard to catch their breath. Hugh Glass was a first-rate man to be with in a fight. He would see Ed Rose many times again over the years to come. He would, a few weeks later, be attacked by a grizzly bear and left for dead by his companions. But he would cling to life and would crawl hundreds of miles, without a weapon, to safety, and would emerge from one of the most unbelievable adventures in the annals of the West. And although they had escaped death this time at the hands of the Aricaras, Hugh Glass would share the last battle with Ed Rose.

13

THE boats dropped down the river to an island. All the goods were transferred to one keelboat and the other was sent down the stream with the men who did not volunteer to remain. Thirty offered to stay, among them nine *voyageurs*. Indian fighting was too hot for the others.

A young man named Jedediah Smith volunteered to go to Andrew Henry at the fort on the Yellowstone for help. Smith's trip across the prairie with only one companion is one of the great stories of adventure and travel of the early West. Jed Smith had been born in New York. At the age of eighteen he went to St. Louis and began to work for Ashley and Henry in 1823. He was on his first trip to the West, a young man still in his early twenties.

Another messenger was sent to Fort Atkinson, almost six hundred miles south, above the mouth of the Platte, requesting help of the army troops stationed there.

General Ashley remained on the island in the river.

Ed Rose was one of the courageous few who stayed with the general.

Three weeks later, on June 22, Colonel Henry Leavenworth from Fort Atkinson, in command of troops near Council Bluffs, left to aid Ashley with two hundred men, two six-pound cannon, several small swivel cannon, and three keelboats.

Joshua Pilcher, the president of the Missouri Fur Company who had recently suffered an even greater disaster than Ashley's earlier losses on the Yellowstone, followed Leavenworth. He was eager to give the Indians a lesson. With forty men, he equipped two boats. One of his weapons was a five-and-a-half-inch howitzer from Fort Atkinson. On the way he engaged about five hundred Yanktons and Sioux who were itching for a fight with the Aricaras to avenge a recent defeat.

Jedediah Smith completed his remarkable trip across the prairie and back. On July 2, he returned to Ashley with Andrew Henry and fifty men. It had been a long hard trip to the Yellowstone.

When the four parties met—Ashley, Henry, Atkinson, and Pilcher—they were organized along military lines. General Ashley nominated nine officers. Edward Rose was one of them and Colonel Leavenworth appointed him an Ensign. Leavenworth, in his report of the expedition, said: "These appointments were merely nominal, and intended only to confer the same privileges and respect on them as were paid to our own officers of the same grade." The forces thus organized under the command of Colonel Leavenworth were called "The Missouri Legion."

The Missouri Legion moved against the Aricaras on August 8. The Sioux with Pilcher made the first contact. There was firing against the Indian village behind its stockade during the next two days. Grey Eyes, an Aricara chief, fell. The morning of August 11, another Aricara chief, Little Soldier, sued for peace. His people had been seriously hurt by the battle. They were alarmed and fearful. They wanted the attack to stop. Would the great white chief send some of his chiefs to the village?

Was this an Aricara trick? There were three thousand Aricaras in the village, with over eight hundred warriors. They were behind strong fortifications. If the white leaders could be killed, the Aricaras might make a quick peace with the Yanktons and the Sioux, and wipe out the soldiers and trappers.

Leavenworth could not take such a chance. He had to make sure the Aricaras were sincere, that their hearts were good, that they spoke with a straight tongue. He could not risk sending all of his leaders into the village. Who would go on such a mission? Ashley had thirty men. Henry had fifty. Pilcher had forty. There were 220 soldiers and their officers.

The leaders held a hurried discussion. There was only one man to go. Edward Rose, a man whose judgment, courage and knowledge of Indians and their language could be trusted.

If General Ashley doubted Rose a short time before, he believed in him now. Rose had fought against the Aricaras for the past three days. He had refused their offer to save himself at the beginning of the battle. He had been their enemy.

Now the black man cradled his rifle in his arm, hoisted his belt so his knife would be within easy reach, and turned toward the Indian village. With the confidence given by knowledge of Indian ways and a courageous heart, he walked, alone, into a village where eight hundred knives might be waiting for him.

The intense drama and the high tension of the moment is put into these commonplace, matter of fact words by Chittenden: "Edward Rose, one of the interpreters, was now sent in and soon returned with the information that the Indians were completely humbled."

14

Eᴅ ʀᴏsᴇ accomplished his mission well, for now eleven Aricara chiefs came out to the military encampment. They signed a treaty with six of the army officers. The Aricaras promised to return General Ashley's property, they agreed not to molest the trappers any more, and both parties promised to live in peace.

But the Indians surrendered only three rifles, one horse, and sixteen robes. In the argument that followed, Rose, the interpreter, took a major part. He was the ears and the voice of both parties. His words expressed what was in the minds and on the tongues of the groups which only the day before had been locked in battle. The Indians said that Grey Eyes had taken most of Ashley's goods. He was now dead, and no more of the property could be found. Indians were not always the silent men they are sometimes pictured. They were often great orators and had an easy and convincing way in an argument.

Again Edward Rose was sent into the village, and

soon Indians came out with more of Ashley's stolen
goods. But all of the property was still not returned
and Rose told Colonel Leavenworth the Indians were
preparing to escape that night. However, no action was
taken, and the next morning the Aricaras were gone.

Pilcher and some others wanted to pursue them, but
Colonel Leavenworth thought it would be better to do
nothing more. Upon his return to Fort Atkinson, he reported:

"The blood of our countrymen has been honorably
avenged, the Aricaras humbled, and in such manner as
will teach them and other Indian tribes to respect the
American name and character."

Pilcher bitterly disputed the Colonel's conclusions
and complained that the expedition against the Aricaras
was a military failure and that the outrages of the Indians would only increase because of the failure to follow and punish them.

Whether it was because of Leavenworth's generosity
or in spite of it, the Aricaras continued to fight trappers
traveling the waters of the Missouri. They murdered
many men unfortunate enough to fall into their
clutches. It was largely because of them, as well as other
Indians along its banks, that Missouri River travel became unpopular and the Oregon Trail up the Platte
River was developed.

Whatever may be said of the total result of the cam-
paign against the Aricaras, in his official report dated

October 20, 1823, to General Atkinson, Colonel Leavenworth placed high value on the services of Edward Rose. Leavenworth reported:

"I had not found any one willing to go into those villages, except a man by the name of Rose, who had the nominal rank of ensign in General Ashley's volunteers. He appeared to be a brave and enterprising man, and was well acquainted with those Indians. He had resided for about three years with them; understood their language, and they were much attached to him. He was with General Ashley when he was attacked. The Indians at that time called to him to take care of himself, before they fired upon General Ashley's party. This was all I knew of the man. I have since heard that he was not of good character. Everything he told us, however, was fully corroborated. He was perfectly willing to go into their villages, and did go in several times."

Here appear traces of an old rumor directed against Rose, a rumor probably arising from Wilson Price Hunt's attitude. But here is a responsible army officer who testifies to the courage, the ability, and the integrity of Edward Rose.

15

Aғтᴇʀ the battle with the Aricaras, General Ashley began to send his men west to carry out his plans for the trapping season. Those who went included men whose vigor and restless courage were equal to the gigantic task of exploring a vast, unknown land, and preparing it for the settlers who would follow them in the decades to come. They included Jedediah Smith, David Jackson, William Sublette, Jim Bridger, James Clyman, Hugh Glass, Thomas Fitzpatrick, and others. Of course, Edward Rose was with them.

Andrew Henry, with a party of about twenty men moved out along the Grand River toward the mouth of the Yellowstone. A month later, Jed Smith at the head of a small group started out from Fort Kiowa. James Clyman, who kept notes of his western travels and who later wrote of his experiences, says there were nine men in the party. Among them were Fitzpatrick, Sublette, and Rose. It is Clyman's narrative that gives us information of the journey and Edward Rose's part in it. Rose was the only one familiar with the country and the Indian language, so we may be sure he played an important part in the day to day progress.

James Clyman was born in Virginia in 1792 on land his father leased from George Washington. As a boy he was in Indian wars, and later he fought in the Black Hawk War in the same company with Abraham Lincoln. He had worked as a farmer and as a surveyor with a son of Alexander Hamilton. He had worked as a clerk for a salt mine before he hired out to Ashley as a clerk for a dollar a day, and he helped his employer enlist trappers, hunters, and boatmen for the trip up the Missouri.

Jed Smith was a devout Christian and a man of fierce courage and untiring energy. He had already proved himself by making his unusual journey to the Yellowstone. Ashley's estimate of the young man is evident in the fact that he made him the captain of the small party now on its way westward. Tom Fitzpatrick, another in the group, was to become one of the most famous of all mountain men and later would serve as the first Indian agent for the Plains Indians.

It is hardly possible to overemphasize the superior qualities of the men who went west for Ashley in 1823. Robert Glass Cleland, in *This Reckless Breed of Men*, says that the roster of Ashley's motley bands "contained the names of a minority who were destined to live for generations in the history and heroic tradition of the

race. . . ." Dale, in the *Ashley-Smith Explorations,* de-
clares they constituted "the most significant group of
continental explorers ever brought together."

The first day the small party moved over a dry,
rolling highland and camped on White Clay Creek,
now known as White River. Their guide warned them
not to drink the water. Later there was no need of
warning. There was no water to drink and they were
told there would be none until the following noon.

The land leveled out and the wide expanse of plain
did not support a single tree as far as the eye could see.
One night, Clyman recorded, they camped ". . . whare
the cactus was so thick that we could scarcely find room
to spred our Blankets. . . ."

They plodded through the heat of the following day,
leading their pack horses. The battle with the Aricaras
had made it impossible to obtain enough of the necessary animals, so the men walked. Long after the sun
had passed mid-point in the sky, the guide pointed
toward a low green cover shimmering in the hot sun.
Their pace quickened as they eagerly approached the
promise of water.

But the pale green leaves that had beckoned them
were withered and shriveled. The stream was dry. Instead of the water they had expected, they found
cracked, parched earth and only ". . . a few Shrubby
oaks to protect us from the scortching sun . . ."

The following day the party became a long, unor-

ganized, straggling line. Then its members moved away
from each other, each searching for water, and they
advanced on a front over a mile wide. To Clyman,
"... it appeared like we might never all collect together
again ..."

Two of the men staggered and fell, unable to go on.
To save them from the burning sun and to conserve
whatever moisture remained in their spent bodies, they
were covered with sand, with only their heads showing
above the surface.

Shortly before the cruel sun fell below the barren
horizon, James Clyman discovered water. "I fired my
gun immedieately," he reports, "and then ran into the
pool arm deep my horse foloin me."

He drank and then fired his gun again to signal for
the other men, and "... one man and horse made their
appearance . . . the horse outran the man plunging
into the water first . . ." Each newcomer to the life-giv-
ing water fired his gun and "Shouted as soon as he could
moisten his mouth and throat Sufficienty to mak a
noise."

Water was carried back two miles to the two men
who had been buried in the sand. After that, two more
days of thirst and starvation took them to the Teton,
or Bad, River where they were able to obtain twenty-
seven fresh horses from Indians. Now each man had
two horses and there were several spares.

They passed the Black Hills and "... again fell into

a tract of county whare no vegetation of any kind existed beeing worn into knobs and gullies and extremely
uneven . . ." Travel became worse than it had been
before and Clyman called the land a "pile of ashes." He
said of the Bad Lands, ". . . it looked a little remarkable
that not a foot of level land could be found, the narrow
revines going in all manner of direction . . ."

Then, quite suddenly, the country changed and they
passed through a pleasant area of pine trees, where
hazel nuts and delicious ripe plums were found. But it
was not to last long. The character of the land changed
again, for ". . . one evening late gowing down a small
stream we came into a Kenyon and pushed ourselves
down so far that our horses had no room to turn. While
looking for a way out it became dark. By unpacking
and leading our animals down over slipery rocks three
of us got down to a nice open glade . . . the rest of the
company remained in the Kenyon without room to lie
down . . ."

After this experience they concluded it was better
not to follow the streams so closely. They moved away,
to the rocky upland, but they were in for more hard
times. ". . . this portion of the mountain furnished our
horses with no food and they began to be verry poor
and weak so we left 3 men and 5 horses behind to re-
cruit."

Captain Jedediah Smith could not afford to discard
the precious trade goods the horses carried, but he

might cache the goods. He could dig a deep dry hole, hide the goods in it, and return for them later. But that would take precious time and there was always a chance that alert Indian eyes might discover the cache and lift the property in it.

Help was needed and Jed Smith knew exactly what to do. He spoke to Edward Rose. Could he go on alone? Could he go to the Crows and get help?

The party was in a desperate condition. Rose nodded. His worried companions watched him hopefully as he prepared to leave.

16

Edward rose turned his face westward and moved toward the distant blue line of mountains that hung low to the land and almost disappeared in the shimmering heat waves rising from the scorched earth. None of the horses, tired and worn from the long days of hard travel, was able to carry him on the trip he faced.

At the first rise of land Rose paused and lifted a hand in farewell. Then he turned and broke into the Indian jog that might, just might, take a strong man to the Crows, but which also might end with a black man's white skeleton shining among the rocks of the Bad Lands.

The party Rose left behind moved slowly in the cool of the early morning and late evening. The men sought refuge from the heat of the day in the shade of bare rocks or leafless willows at the edge of dry water beds. The time was rapidly approaching when the horses would not be able to move, when the trade goods would have to be left behind, when it would be a deadly strug-

gle for the men to save themselves, when the investment of Ashley and Henry would be lost, when failure
now lurking in the desert wastes would stand in their
midst.

Jed Smith was attacked by a grizzly bear. His scalp
was cruelly torn. He was clawed and cut to the point
of death. James Clyman cut away his hair, and sewed
the torn face and scalp with a needle and thread.

Slowly, painfully, the party moved on, hoping that
Ed Rose had not been felled by a grizzly, praying that
the big Negro would find help for them.

Jim Clyman saw a shining black mountain with sheer
walls of smooth slate. At its base were rock-hard trees,
petrified ages before. He was amazed at wood and bark
that seemed to be of stone. Several years later when he
met Black Harris, the old trapper told him that if he
had gone farther he would have seen a whole forest
that was petrified. Black Harris was a grizzled mountain man who had a long career in the beaver trade. He
was one of the men who excelled at spinning a yarn.
The tale he told Clyman was embellished and has been
told around a thousand camp fires.

"That entire forest was petrified," said Black Harris.
"Not only the tree trunks, but the branches too. Even
the leaves."

Harris warmed up to the tale. "Not only that,
neither," he continued. "There was birds there that was
petrified. Frozen into stone. And their mouths was

78 EDWARD ROSE

open, jest like they was singin', when they was turned
into stone. An' do you know, them woods was filled
with the most beautiful music, because the songs they
sang was still there, petrified, jest like everything else."

Now it was October of 1823, and the heat of the past
few weeks was gone. Cold came, and snow. The pain of
heat and the burning sun became the torture of freezing
winds and the lash of blown snow.

The horses fell more often and moved more slowly.
Where was Ed Rose? Had he fallen prey to one of the
numerous hazards of the West? How were the three
men faring who had been too exhausted to continue
and who had been left behind?

Suddenly dull, glassy eyes were lit bright with hope,
and yet with fear. Hope, because the long line of horsemen they saw approaching might bring help. Yet fear,
because the horsemen might be searching for scalps and
the wealth the exhausted expedition possessed.

Then, as the distance closed, as the figures became
larger, they could see that the man in the lead was a
broad-shouldered, muscular man. The color of his skin
was darker than the Indians who followed him.

When he drew closer, they saw his black face was
disfigured by a cut nose and by an ugly scar on his forehead. To the exhausted trappers, he looked like an
angel, a rescuing angel. He was Ed Rose with an escort
of Crow Indians and with fresh horses.

Rose went back for the three men and five horses

that had been too weak to keep up with the party. Water and food revived them and they soon joined the group. The merchandise was loaded on the fresh horses. While Wilson Price Hunt had carried a burden of fear of Edward Rose, neither Jed Smith nor his companions had such doubts.

Captain Smith gave Rose the valuable goods to carry into the Crow country where it would be safe from Blackfeet or other prairie raiders. Rose, with the heavily loaded fresh horses went ahead, to safety in Absaroka, the land of the Crows. The rest of the party followed more slowly with the exhausted horses. The expedition was saved.

It is too bad that Wilson Price Hunt didn't know how to recognize the right man for the job he had to do. He might have been more successful.

17

For many years the English and French had traded and trapped in the Columbia River country and on the upper Missouri River. Their routes from the East were along the St. Lawrence River, the Great Lakes, and the Canadian lakes and streams. A handful of adventurous Americans—Edward Rose, Ezekial Williams, Andrew Henry, William Ashley, Manuel Lisa, and others—had gone to the Rocky Mountains from the Mississippi. There had been a few military explorations. Lieutenant Zebulon Montgomery Pike had explored the country along the Arkansas River to the mountains in 1806. A military and scientific expedition to the Yellowstone was attempted in 1819. (It was a failure, progressing no further than the neighborhood of Fort Lisa, near the present site of the city of Omaha, Nebraska.) In 1820, Major Stephen Long followed the South Fork of the Platte to the mountains.

The power of the United States had not been carried to the remote regions, and the American fur trade made its way alone, unaided in any substantial fashion by the government.

There were restless, bold men who were coming to know the West. Ashley's expeditions of 1822, 1823, and 1824 had shown the value and importance of the country west of the Mississippi. Such men were interested in furs, but through them the news spread that the vast space was desirable and even necessary to the full development of the nation.

Trappers and frontier settlements agitated for government help, not merely to impress the Indians, but also to counteract British influence along the frontier. Yet without assistance, trappers had continued their work and had broken the trails for an eager but hesitant nation to follow.

In 1825, General Henry Atkinson and Major Benjamin O'Fallon were commissioned to journey to the Yellowstone country and make treaties with the Indian tribes in the upper Missouri Valley. The expedition was well directed. The Commissioners needed more than soldiers, weapons, boats, horses, and money. They needed guides and interpreters, for without them, no expedition had a chance of success. One of the best was engaged. Edward Rose.

They left Fort Atkinson on May 16, 1825, with 476 troops in the group. Forty men on horseback, under the command of Lieutenant Armstrong went with Rose by land. The rest of the men and supplies moved up the river on nine boats. They were named *Buffalo, Elk, White Bear, Otter, Racoon, Beaver, Mink* and *Muskrat.* The ninth boat was the *Lafayette,* the suttler's boat which carried supplies for the personal needs of the troops which were not furnished by the army.

General Atkinson had devised paddle wheels for the boats which were operated by man power. This new form of propulsion was in addition to oars, poles, sails, and cordelle. (The cordelle was a rope attached to a mast which was used by the men to pull the boats upstream.) Eight to twelve miles a day was considered good distance, although on favorable days they made more. On Sunday, June 4, Ed Rose visited the boats to say that Captain Armstrong's party had reached the Ponca Indians ten days before. He told Atkinson they had found very little game and he returned to the horsemen with a supply of pork from the boats' stores. Sometimes the best of hunters had trouble finding game on the prairie.

On Sunday, June 18, Rose and two soldiers were assigned to go in search of the Cheyenne Indians and bring them to the river to discuss a treaty. On the first day two of their horses escaped and returned to the camp on the river. One of the two soldiers went back for them.

The boats were to meet Captain Armstrong's party at the mouth of the Teton River. Ed Rose had done his work well. The Ogalallas were nearby, six miles up the river. Another tribe was thirty miles away and the Cheyennes were eighty miles up the Teton. Now they were all coming to the council with the Commissioners, the representatives of the Great White Father far away in Washington.

The land party was busy. Captain Armstrong and Lieutenant Waters, with soldiers and interpreters, went to escort the Indians to the council. Edward Rose was with them.

18

Rose led Lieutenant Water's party to the Cheyennes. On their return they joined the other groups and proceeded toward the mouth of the Teton, the Negro leading the way.

He topped a small knoll, drew his horse to a halt, and stood like a statue, silhouetted against the summer sky. Those who followed drew up beside him in a long line from left to right. They saw some brown spots moving on the hillside across the narrow valley. Some of the soldiers may never have seen such animals, but the Indians and Ed Rose recognized them at once. They were buffalo. Eleven buffalo.

There on the opposite hill was Fourth of July dinner for almost five hundred soldiers. Ed Rose spoke to Lieutenant Waters. The officer nodded, and Rose turned toward the Indians. He made a few sharp gestures. An excited murmer ran through the crowd. Chee-ho-carte was going for the buffalo alone. It would be a good show.

Ed Rose checked the direction of the wind. Buffalo did not have especially keen eyesight, but they had a remarkably alert sense of smell. The scent of a hunter borne to them on the breeze would send them scattering.

Ed pressed his knees against his mount. In a few minutes he was in a gully that straggled through the fold between the hills. He dismounted, hobbled his horse, and gathered some branches from bushes growing from the broken edge of the gash in the earth that separated the rising land on either side.

He thrust the branches through his belt, his headband, and the straps holding his shot bag and powder horn. To the watchers at the crest of the knoll, it seemed that a bush began moving up the slope toward the eleven buffalo bulls grazing on the hillside. Slowly the bush moved. Slowly, steadily.

When would Rose fire? If he went too close the animals would discover him and run. The moving bush stopped. A puff of smoke rose from it. A few seconds later those watching heard the crack of a rifle and saw one of the buffalo bulls sink to the ground. A moment later—long enough for a good man with a gun to reload and aim—there was another puff of smoke, another distant report of rifle fire, and another crumbling buffalo.

Each time the rifle fired, the remaining bulls raised

their heads. They saw nothing, smelled nothing, but their nervousness increased.

When the fifth fell, the rest began to move away, sniffing, ears pricked to catch another warning sound. Hesitating, their eyes peering from under shaggy brows, then trotting, with heads turning this way and that, they tried to find the source of the danger.

The big beasts did not know what was wrong, but some instinct warned them, and they broke into a mad gallop. But they were not yet safe. Another puff of smoke broke into bloom above the clump of branches on the distant hillside and another buffalo's legs went limp. He fell to the ground and lay still.

The clerk who kept the journal of the Atkinson-O'Fallon Yellowstone expedition made the following entries:

"Thursday 30 June. Rose, an interpreter, one of the party, we understand, covered himself with bushes and crawled into the gang of 11 Bulls and shot down 6 on the same ground before the others ran off.

Friday 1st July. Today the 6 Buffalo killed by Rose yesterday were bro't into camp and weighed net 3,300— The flesh was issued to the Troops making an issue of 4½ days at 1½ Lbs of rations, besides the officers Messes were furnished with an abundance."

19

IT WAS not possible for General Atkinson or Major O'Fallon or the other officers and men to talk to the Indians without the aid of an interpreter. Although Rose was not the only interpreter available, we may be sure his years of life with the Indians, his knowledge of their customs, culture, traditions, and language were not wasted. His duties involved more than searching out Indian tribes and encouraging them to come to a council with the Commissioners.

He sat at the right hand of the Commissioners and the army officers and, by his skill and knowledge, made sure the minds of the representatives of the United States and of the Indians met and found common understanding. He was serving his country in a highly technical and extremely important fashion. He was at the sensitive heart of the negotiations. Whether an interpreter is always mentioned in the official journal of the expedition or not, we may be sure one was there, and we may be equally sure there was a good chance it was Ed Rose.

The journal of the expedition for the following six days reveals typical activity of the party, activity of the kind that went on during the entire summer and fall. It was difficult work of a delicate nature, for the goal was to peacefully impress the Indians with the importance and the sovereignty of the United States.

On July 2, the Ogalallas, led by Chief Standing Buffalo visited the expedition to inquire where he should pitch his nation's lodges. The chief, a dignified man, led a band of 250 warriors who were housed in 110 tipis. Rose and four soldiers were dispatched to meet another band under Chief Fireheart that was expected at the meeting, and to see if buffalo could be found.

On July 3, news arrived that another group of Ogalallas and a village of Cheyennes were on their way to the council. A message also came from a band which the clerk of the expedition referred to as Siones. They, too, would arrive the next day. In the afternoon of July 4, the Ogalalla camp entertained the Commissioners and army officers at a boiled dog dinner, with much Indian ceremony. The Cheyennes and Siones were present, seated on buffalo robes and beaver skins. All joined in smoking the peace pipe.

The brigade was reviewed in the presence of the Indians on July 5. The large cannon were mounted on wheels and drawn by horses at full speed over the prairie. The Indians were struck with a great awe at the military display. In the evening they were awed even more when they witnessed the setting off of twenty rockets by Lieutenant Holmes. (This was the same Lieutenant Holmes who, three years later, wrote *The Five Scalps,* the story of Ed Rose.)

The following day the council resumed and treaties were signed with Ogalallas, Cheyennes, and Siones. The chiefs were given horses, holsters, pistols, and swords. In the evening High-backed Wolf, the principal chief of the Cheyennes, gave General Atkinson a handsome mule, with a rope and saddle. The clerk who wrote the journal observed that the chief was "one of the most dignified & elegant looking men I ever saw." In the evening "Lt. Holmes threw 6 shells from the Howitzer in the presense of the Indians, they exploded handsomely & made a deep impression upon these savages.'

Early on the morning of July 7, the boats moved up the river. The wind was fair and both sails and paddle wheels were used. They "ran up a stretch of 1½ miles in view of more than 3,000 Indians who lined the shore." In a ten-hour day they went twenty miles. That evening thirty horses were sent back to Council Bluffs. Thirteen horses were kept for packing meat for the hard-working troops.

Thereafter Captain Armstrong's men, moving on foot, served as flankers. Ed Rose was with these soldiers who guarded the flanks of the expedition. The inter-

preter, the voice of the Commissioners and Indians at
the councils, now became the ears and eyes necessary to
protect from surprise attack. The men on the flanks
would receive the first charge of any enemy.

And so, a typical week passed. Treaties were signed
with three Indian tribes. The name and the power of
the United States was being carried, in peace, to the
Indians of the plains.

20

A MONTH later, on August 4, 1825, an incident occurred that brought out the courage in Edward Rose
and revealed once again his fearlessness and dominat-
ing personality.

The Crows had come to the council meeting. The
brigade had appeared under arms and passed in review
with the artillery mounted on wheels and drawn by
horses. It was a colorful display. After the review, the
soldiers were released. The council met and a treaty
was signed and peace seemed secure.

The Crows had two Iroquois prisoners whom they
refused to set free upon the request of the Commissioners. While the subject was being discussed with
some heat, Crow warriors went to the cannon and
stuffed the touch holes with dirt. This would prevent
their being fired. Then, they began demanding presents, and attempted to take the gifts before they were
actually offered.

Major O'Fallon saw the disturbance and rushed to

break it up. Some of the lesser chiefs also came to the scene and began to share in the tussle for presents. Major O'Fallon drew his pistol and struck a chief with it. A tumult arose. Six hundred Crow warriors, fully armed, swirled around the center of the melee. Their voices expressed their rage in excited sound.

Violence was beating within each Crow breast. They were ready for a fight. The peace treaty and the pleasant words at the council were forgotten. A fight would result in loss of life that would not be forgotten for many years. The whole expedition was on the brink of failure.

The tension marked by a rising crescendo of angry voices was ready to break. It seemed that nothing could stop it. Anything could spark frightening violence at such a moment. Could anything quiet it?

Ed Rose, standing behind Major O'Fallon, stooped and seized a gun from a pile lying at the feet of the chiefs. He raised it and swung the barrel so vigorously that several warriors felt its sting. The milling crowd backed away, making a wide circle, with Rose in its center.

He was face to face with Long Hair, one of the principal chiefs, the gun raised, ready it seemed, to make Long Hair its next victim. Lieutenant Holmes was there, and wrote of the episode in *The Five Scalps.*

"One foot was on the pile of muskets, to prevent the Indians from taking any from it, and the other was on the ground. . . . Though to all appearance, he would have died with a hundred wounds, had the storm burst, still his eye gleamed with triumphant satisfaction. There was an expression about his mouth, slightly curved and compressed, and a little smiling at the curves, indicative of a delirium of delight—his eye, his mouth, the position of his head, and scars on his forehead and nose all united in forming a general expression, that, of itself, seemed to paralize the nerves of every Indian before him. Once seen, the mind forever retains it. I have often, and often, dreamed of the look and position of that man in that Council scene. It has arisen before me when alone in my room, and when surrounded by a crowd. It distinctly exhibited a compound of every passion and feeling in the human heart, except mercy."

But the Lieutenant was wrong in at least one respect. Mercy was there, too, or perhaps it was intelligence or absolute knowledge of Indian ways.

The excited shouting died down and a mountain of silence settled on the enraged braves. Six hundred Indians were subdued by a single man.

Jim Beckwourth, the famous Negro mountain man, then on his way home with General William Ashley after his first trip to the mountains, heard the story a few weeks later from General Atkinson. In his autobiography Beckwourth says:

"When this occurrence reached the ears of the Indian warriors, they became perfectly infuriated, and prepared for instant attack. General Atkinson pacified them through Rose, who was one of the best interpreters ever known in the whole Indian country."

The incident passed into folklore and Washington Irving many years later got the story from an old trapper. Irving tells us that Rose "laid so vigorously about him with the barrel, that he soon put the whole throng to flight. Luckily, as no lives had been lost, this sturdy rib-roasting calmed the fury of the Crows, and the tumult ended without serious consequences."

This episode in the life of Edward Rose is the best documented of any that has come down to us. All versions of the story agree that he was a man of unquestioned and undoubted courage.

The Atkinson-O'Fallon expedition of 1825 was a success. The Commissioners had found all the tribes they hoped to, except two. They had everywhere made satisfactory treaties. They left with the Indians a strong impression of the friendship and power of the United States.

The interpreters and guides of such an expedition carried an enormous responsibility. Success or failure depended on them to a great extent. It is clear that Edward Rose is entitled to a firm and high place among the heroes who took the first steps in the taming of an unknown wilderness.

21

THE warfare between the Crows and the Blackfeet, and indeed, between most Indian tribes, was constantly sparked and kept aflame by horse stealing expeditions against each other. There were no precise boundaries between Indian tribes but, in general, the Blackfoot lands were north of the Missouri, while the heart of Absaroka, the land of the Crows, was in the valley of the Big Horn River. Herds of buffalo and other game moved over wide areas and the Indians followed them. Hunters and war parties were always on the move.

It is quite clear that the Crows received the trappers as friends. The Missouri River route to the West was abandoned largely because of the bloody ways of the Blackfeet as well as other river Indians. One of the most powerful influences upon the Crows was Edward Rose. His authority existed for almost three decades after 1807, the years of the beginning and the rapid growth of the fur industry, the years when the small, weak

fingers of the sovereignty of the United States first
reached toward the great West.

Rose's influence was shared with that of James Beckwourth from 1826 on. These two Negroes did a remarkable job in keeping relative peace along the western
reaches of the Platte. Jim Beckwourth, too, lived with
the Crows for many years, was greatly respected and
became a chief of the nation. If the Crows had been
as vicious toward the trappers as the Blackfeet, the
thrust of United States control of the West could have
been held back for many years.

Jim Beckwourth realized that his efforts in keeping
the Crows at peace with the trappers were worth more
than the efforts of a regiment of soldiers. The work Ed
Rose did was probably even more valuable because
he got there first and stayed longer. An Ed Rose filled
with hatred for his fellow trappers would have made
the way very hard indeed. His friendship and his help
in the critical area between the Yellowstone and the
Platte rivers, the gateway to the West, was a matter of
first importance.

We do not know where Rose was at all times, or the
precise details of what he did every moment. We are
usually limited to glimpses of him when he stepped out
of his life with Indians and acted as guide and interpreter. But Zenas Leonard had an opportunity to see
Rose with the Crows. He reveals one of the reasons
Chee-ho-carte was so much admired by the Indians,

who, above all things, respected courage. Indians also admired a winner, especially a winner against their ancient enemies, the Blackfeet.

Zenas Leonard had been born in Pennsylvania in 1809. He had a grade school education and spent his early years farming, clerking in a store, and hunting. He seized the opportunity for the adventuresome life of a fur trapper and left for the mountains with a small trapping party in April, 1831. In the winter of 1838-9 he wrote of his experiences. His story, written within four years after his return from the mountains, gives us a clear picture of some incidents in the life of Edward Rose.

Zenas' first glimpse of Ed came out of the theft of five fine hunting horses. The theft took place in November on the headwaters of the Colorado River. Leonard's group followed the horse theives over the Continental Divide to the junction of the Stinking River and the Big Horn. Here, they met Chee-ho-carte who told them he had come to the mountains with Lewis and Clark, a bit of typical mountain man exaggeration. (The man Leonard met could not have been York, William Clark's Negro servant who went to the Pacific many years before with the first and greatest expedition and was the only Negro in the Lewis and Clark party.)

The trappers got their horses back and Zenas reveals something of the quality and character of Rose.

"In this village we found a Negro man. . . . He has acquired a correct knowledge of their manner of living, and speaks their language fluently. He had rose to be quite a considerable character, or chief, in their village . . .

"After informing the Negro of our stolen horses, he told us that they had them, and that the reason they were taken from us was because we were found in their enemies' country, and that they supposed we were going to trade them guns &c. By giving the chiefs some trifling presents our horses were produced in as good trim as when they left us."

The following November, Leonard's party visited the land of the Crows again, and once more he found cause to comment about the Negro chief.

"This man we found to be of as great advantage to us now as on former occasions, as he has become thoroughly acquainted with their language, method of transacting their public and private business, and considered of great value by the Indians. He enjoys prefect peace and satisfaction, and has everything that he desired at his own command."

In Rose's courteous treatment of Leonard's party we find a measure of the error of Wilson Price Hunt over twenty years before. Mr. Leonard makes it evident that Hunt's offer of half a year's pay, three traps, and a horse would be meaningless to a man in Chee-ho-carte's position. The Negro's power is also made evident by Lieutenant Holmes' story, for he says:

"He was consulted on all occasions; his word was law, and, he well knew how to give it in an elevated tone. Nothing could be done without 'Chee-ho-carte' pronounced them good."

Another glimpse Zenas Leonard gives us of Ed Rose while living with the Crows involves an incident somewhat similar to the fight with the Minnatarees. It is not unlikely there were two such incidents and perhaps even more, when it is remembered that warfare was continuous.

Zenas Leonard says it took place on November 20, 1834, somewhere in the neighborhood of the Big Horn and Wind rivers, when five hundred Crows started out on a buffalo hunt. Zenas and his companions followed them as "This was a favorable opportunity for me to gratify my curiosity in seeing this kind of sport."

The Crows turned from their buffalo hunt when they saw other Indians advancing. The keen-eyed braves soon recognized the strangers as ". . . their implacable enemies, the Blackfeet tribe. This was enough. War was now their only desire, and our Indians advanced towards their enemies as fast as the speed of their horses would admit. . . ."

The Blackfeet, to escape battle on the prairie, climbed to a rocky hillside where they found a ledge of rocks three or four feet high, shaped in the form of a horseshoe. They added to the strength of their natural fort by piling up more stones, tree trunks, and branches, so that they had a decided advantage over the Crows.

The news spread and the whole Crow village came to the scene. Two hundred Crow warriors mounted an attack. The fire from the makeshift fort compelled them to retreat.

The Crows attacked by riding full speed along the top of the ridge, firing as they passed. They threw themselves on the sides of their horses until nothing was exposed to the enemy except one arm and one leg. Still, they were not protected, for the horses were easy targets for the Blackfeet.

Some of the Crows were willing to abandon the battle, but another attack was made. War whoops made the echoes bounce off the rock walls and two hundred Crows sounded like a thousand angry devils.

The attack failed. So did the attacks that followed. The Crows became overwhelmed by despair. There seemed to be no way to reach the Blackfeet in their natural fort ". . . when the Negro, who has been heretofore mentioned, and who had been in company with us, advanced a few steps towards the Crows and ascended a rock from which he addressed the Crow warriors in the most earnest and impressive manner. . . ."

Many Indians were impressive orators and skilled in argument. Obviously Edward Rose had these talents also. "He told them that they had been here making

a great noise, as if they could kill the enemy by it. . . .
He told them their hearts were small, and that they
were cowardly—that they acted more like squaws than
men, and were not fit to defend their hunting ground."

Zenas describes an impassioned speech in which Rose
used every argument calculated to persuade an Indian.
Then he made the greatest argument of all; it was an
example of courage, which Indians could not resist. As
Zenas tells it,

"The old Negro continued in this strain until they
became greatly animated, and told them that if the red
man was afraid to go among his enemy, he would show
them that a black man was not, and he leaped from the
rock on which he had been standing, and looking neither to the right nor to the left, made for the fort as fast
as he could run."

The Indians followed, inspired both by his words
and his action. With his leadership, victory came in
moments.

Here, Zenas Leonard gives us a picture of Edward
Rose, of Chee-ho-carte, bringing victory to his adopted
people when victory seemed remote. Little wonder the
Sparrow Hawk people so loved and respected him.

Here, also, we see Edward Rose engaged in the business of discouraging the dangerous Blackfeet from en-
croaching on Crow territory and thereby blocking the
westward movement of the trappers.

22

IN THE years following Ashley's journeys to the beaver streams of the Rockies, more and more trappers followed. The young men and boys became mature mountain men.

The time for Ed Rose to die had come. The man who had faced death as a daily diet for almost a quarter of a century met it at long last.

It is not clear how it happened, or when, or where. On some points there is agreement. Hugh Glass, an old friend, was with him—Hugh Glass, who had faced the Aricaras on a sand bar with Ed ten years before. Then, no lethal bullets found them. But the Aricaras had moved from their old haunts on the Missouri and had foraged west, and Aricaras fired the guns that cut down Glass and Rose.

One story has it that Ed Rose and Hugh Glass met death in the explosion of a powder barrel during a flaming Aricara attack on the prairie. Another, coming from Jim Beckwourth who was a chief of the Crows,

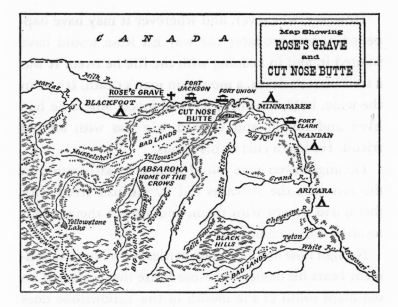

tells of an ambush by the Aricaras as the two men walked on the frozen Yellowstone on a trip down the river to the Absaroka.

An untold tale lies behind early records that Rose's grave was at the junction of the Milk and the Missouri rivers. Chittenden, who wrote his history in 1902, repeats the account of death by gunpowder explosion, but he adds:

"Whether this story is true or not, the locality of the occurrence is most likely wrong, for Rose was buried on the banks of the Missouri nearly opposite to the mouth of Milk river. On any of the old steamboat itineraries of the Missouri river may be seen among the names in that vicinity, 'Rose's Grave'."

However, whenever, and wherever it may have happened, it was probably the way Ed Rose would have wanted it, and in keeping with the life he lived. It was a trail blazer's death, a mountain man's death. It was in the wide, bold, beautiful land he loved, where he had lived and fought and worked. He was with an old friend. He had a rifle in his hands.

He might even have found some grim satisfaction in the fact that the Aricaras did it. He had lived with them, had fought with them, and against them, as his loyalties had demanded.

No sign now marks his last battle. No place or monument bears his name. Cut Nose Butte that appeared on old maps south of the mouth of the Yellowstone does not appear on modern maps. The West where Ed Rose blazed the trails seems to have forgotten him. But if men have forgotten, the trails he made remain. His footprints were the marks others followed and still follow.

The turmoil of exploration, the stretch of the long arm of sovereignty, the clash of cultures bring strange results. It is always a long, hard road to something better, and something better must come when serious energetic people strive for it and use all their talents to the fullest extent possible. It is not easy.

A man does his part if he does all he can do with the abilities he has, if he strives each day to do a good job, whatever his job may be.

Ed Rose helped his nation move forward. He was one of the first to face the western wilderness, and one of the best. What he did made it better and easier for those who followed and who will follow.

Selected Bibliography

Adams, James Truslow, editor. *Atlas of American History*. New York: Charles Scribner's Sons, 1943

Alter, J. Cecil. *James Bridger*. Salt Lake City: Shepard Book Company, 1925

Bonner, T. D. *The Life and Adventures of James P. Beckwourth*. New York: Harper & Brothers, 1856

California Historical Society Quarterly, Vols. 4, 5, 6. *James Clyman's Narration*. Charles L. Camp, editor. San Francisco: California Historical Society, 1925

Carrington, Margaret Irvin Sullivant. *Ab-sa-ra-ka, Land of Massacre*. Henry B. Carrington, editor. Philadelphia: J. B. Lippincott & Co., 1878

Chittenden, Hiram Martin. *The American Fur Trade of the Far West*. New York: F. P. Harper, 1902 (Academic Reprints, Stanford, 1954)

Clyman, James. *James Clyman, Frontiersman*. Charles E. Camp, editor. Portland, Oregon: The Champaeg Press, 1960

Coyner, David H. *The Lost Trappers*. Cincinnati: Anderson, Gates & Wright, 1859

Dale, Herrison Clifford. *The Ashley-Smith Explorations*. Cleveland: A. H. Clark Co., 1918

De Voto, Bernard. *Across the Wide Missouri*. Boston: Houghton, Mifflin Company, 1947

Dictionary of American Biography, Vol. XVI. New York: Charles Scribner & Sons, 1935

Ewers, John C. *Artists of the Old West*. New York: Doubleday & Company, 1965

Ghent, W. J. *The Early Far West*. New York: Tudor Publishing Company, 1936

Greenbie, Sydney. *Furs to Furrows.* Caldwell, Idaho: The Caxton Printers, Ltd., 1939

Gregg, Josiah. *Commerce of the Prairies.* New York: H. G. Langley, 1844

Hafen, LeRoy, and Ghent W. J. *Broken Hand, The Life Story of Thomas Fitzpatrick, Chief of the Mountain Men.* Denver: The Old West Publishing Co., 1931

Hodge, Frederick Webb. *Handbook of American Indians.* Washington, D. C.: Bureau of American Ethnology, Bulletin 30, 1907

Holmes, Captain Ruben. *The Five Scalps.* Weekly Reveille, St. Louis, Missouri, vol. 5, No. 3; July 17, 24, 1848

Hulbert, Archer B. *The Paths of Inland Commerce.* New Haven: The Yale University Press, 1921

Irving, Washington. *Astoria.* Philadelphia: Carey, Lea & Blanchard, 1836

———. *The Rocky Mountains.* Philadelphia: Carey, Lea & Blanchard, 1837

Jones, Evan and Dale L. Morgan. *Trappers and Mountain Men.* New York: American Heritage Publishing Company, 1961

Leonard, Zenas. *Adventures of Zenas Leonard, Fur Trader.* Edited by John C. Ewers. Norman, Oklahoma: University of Oklahoma Press, 1959

Morgan, Dale L. *Jedediah Smith and the Opening of the West.* New York: The Bobbs-Merrill Company, Inc., 1953

———. *The West of William Ashley.* Denver: The Old West Publishing Co., 1964

Neihardt, John G. *The Splendid Wayfaring.* New York: The Macmillan Company, 1920

Nichols, Roger L. *General Henry Atkinson.* Norman, Oklahoma: University of Oklahoma Press, 1965

North Dakota Historical Society Quarterly, Vol. 4, No. 1, October, 1929, *Journal of the Atkinson-O'Fallon Expedition,* edited by Russell Reid and Clell G. Gannon. Bismarck, North Dakota: Historical Society of North Dakota

Oglesby, Richard Edward. *Manuel Lisa and the Opening of the Fur Trade.* Norman, Oklahoma: University of Oklahoma Press, 1963

Parkman, Francis. *The California and Oregon Trail.* New York: G. P. Putnam, 1849

Ross, Alexander. *The Fur Hunters of the Far West.* Edited by
Kenneth Spaulding, Norman, Oklahoma: University of Okla-
homa Press, 1956
——. *The Fur Hunters of the Far West.* London; Smith, Elder &
Co., 1855
Ross, Marvin C. *The West of Alfred Jacob Miller.* Norman, Okla-
homa: University of Oklahoma Press, 1951
Skinner, Constance L. *Adventurers of Oregon.* New Haven: The
Yale University Press, 1920
South Dakota Historical Collections, Vol. 1. Official correspondence
pertaining to the Leavenworth Expedition of 1823 (Notes by
Doane Robinson), compiled by the State Historical Society.
Aberdeen, South Dakota: News Printing Co., 1902
Stuart, Robert. *The Discovery of the Oregon Trail,* edited by Phillip
Ashton Rollins. New York: Charles Scribner's Sons, 1935
Vestal, Stanley. *Jim Bridger, Mountain Man.* New York: William
Morrow & Company, 1946
——. *Kit Carson.* Boston: Houghton, Mifflin Company, 1928
Victor, Frances Fuller. *The River of the West.* Hartford: Columbian
Book Company, 1871

Index

The Author

Harold W. Felton, a lawyer by profession, has long been interested in American folklore, and the first of his widely acclaimed books was an anthology of legends about Paul Bunyan. Since that time he has pursued folk heroes and tall tales with enthusiasm, and his stories for young people, about Pecos Bill, John Henry, Fire-Fightin' Mose, Bowleg Bill, and Sergeant O'Keefe rank him as a master yarnspinner.

In A HORSE NAMED JUSTIN MORGAN and WILLIAM PHIPS AND THE TREASURE SHIP, Mr. Felton dealt with facts that seemed like tall tales—history that was "almost too good to be true." In researching JIM BECKWOURTH, NEGRO MOUNTAIN MAN and the story of Edward Rose, he discovered the same sort of material—biographies more astounding than fiction.

Born in the Midwest, this popular author lives in New York City where he devotes his leisure time to writing.

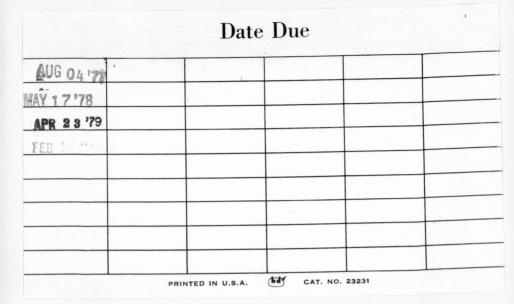